TEARS

OF

BLOOD

TEARS
OF
BLOOD

A Korean POW's Fight for Freedom, Family, and Justice

By Young-Bok Yoo

Translated by Paul T. Kim

Tears of Blood – A Korean POW's Fight for Freedom, Family, and Justice
Young-Bok Yoo

Translated by Paul Taewan Kim from Mr. Young-Bok Yoo's autobiography, printed in
Korea as *Starry Nights in Hell* (2010) and reprinted as *Two Fateful Days* (2011).

For Korean copyright and permissions, please contact:
Won Books
277-12 Sosa-bon-3-dong, Sosa-ku, Bucheon-si, Gyeonggi-do, Korea
Phone: +82 (32) 349-7391
won_books@naver.com

Printed by Korean War POW Affairs – USA

Edited by David Alzofon, thirdpersonpov@hotmail.com

Book design by Frankie Frey, chameleongraphicssite.com

All photographs © 2012 by Won Books

First printed July 2012

10 9 8 7 6 5 4 3 2

ISBN 978-1479383856

For cataloging information, please refer to the Korean version of the autobiography:

    Library of Congress Control Number 2011484779
    Yu, Yŏng-bok, 1930-
    Unmyŏng ŭi tu nal : 6. 25 Kukkun kwihwan yongsa Yu Yŏng-bok ŭi Pukhan
    t'alch'ulgi

PRAISE FOR TEARS OF BLOOD

In this excellent, clear and highly readable translation by Paul Kim, still in high school, we learn the moving story of Young-Bok Yoo, whose life exemplifies the tragedies and divisions of Korea during and after the Korean War. This book provides much honest, probing insight into North Korea, where Mr. Yoo lived for decades, and the moving story of his ultimate return to the South. This book could have been a political tract; instead it is an eyewitness account of a gripping and illuminating history.

> — Bruce Cumings, Chairman of the History Department at the University of Chicago, and the author of *Korea's Place in the Sun.*

Tears of Blood: A Korean POW's Fight for Freedom, Family, and Justice, written by Young-Bok Yoo and carefully translated by Paul T. Kim, is required reading for those who care about history, particularly the history of our own times, about human rights, and about the almost unbelievable power of the human being to survive with dignity even under intolerable conditions.

Tears of Blood is Young-Bok Yoo's account of his fifty-year ordeal as a South Korean held prisoner of war in North Korea. Against international conventions of war, he was, as were the other South Korean prisoners, denied repatriation, exploited as a laborer and surveyor in the mines, subjected to harsh political, social, and personal conditions, weakened by tuberculosis, famine, and privations of every kind, and nearly broken by the suffering of his family. "Tears of blood" is in fact a Korean phrase for the agony of witnessing the suffering of those one loves, and despite the brutality Mr. Yoo endured himself, his strongest expressions of grief are for those he loved, some in South Korea from whom he was forcibly separated, and those of the family he formed in North Korea, who suffered with him or who suffered because of his status as a POW.

Though this is not a story with a "happy ending," it does end with Mr. Yoo's daring escape--after five decades--from North Korea and his return to South Korea, a place changed beyond his comprehension, but his home. There, reunited with his surviving family members, he set himself the task of writing his story --for himself, for the 60,000 other South Korean POW's whose stories would echo his but are lost, and for the few of those 60,000 prisoners who still may be alive and living against their will in North Korea.

There is a second story present in this book as well: the story of Paul T. Kim, a young Korean-American, only sixteen when he completed this translation, a task he was enabled to do because his Korean grandmother persisted in bringing him to full fluency in the Korean language. He found Mr. Yoo's story so compelling that he has translated it so that English readers have access to this historical document and what the translator calls "the fading story" of South Korean POW's.

The narrative is simple and unadorned as is appropriate for the grim experience it recounts. With useful explanatory notes provided by the translator and with references to corroborating witnesses, the book adds credibly to our knowledge of a war not given a great deal of attention and reveals the plight of the POW's we seldom hear about. Moreover, the devotion, work, and achievement of the young translator augment our understanding of the concept of heritage.

I strongly endorse the publication of *Tears of Blood*.

— Shirley Clay Scott, former Dean of the School of Arts and Sciences, Hunter College.

Korea has an abundance of human tragedy and international injustice in modern times that has never been fully unfolded to the world. This autobiography by Young-Bok Yoo, a former South Korean POW, abandoned in North Korea for decades, so painful and sad as it may be, is only the tip of the iceberg, one of the countless stories of suffering in North Korea. The story behind this excellent translation, by Paul Kim who is still in high school, is itself an inspiring one for young people who wish to act against injustice.

— Sang Hun Kim, Chairman, Database Center for North Korean Human Rights, and Asian Hero 2003, TIME Magazine Asia.

CONTENTS

INTRODUCTION

The Korean War was fought from June 1950 to July 1953 between the Soviet-backed Democratic People's Republic of Korea (North Korea) and the American-backed Republic of Korea (South Korea). Over 2.5 million people perished during the bloody civil war.

In the aftermath, over 60,000 South Korean soldiers captured by North Korea did not return home. While never accounting for individual captives by name, North Korea claimed that they had let all of the POWs go, and that any prisoner who stayed in the North had voluntarily defected to the Communist side.

Then, starting in 1994, a trickle of South Korean POWs began to escape from North Korea and arrive in the South. These individuals— youths when they disappeared but elderly when they returned—brought with them harrowing tales of imprisonment, oppression, abuse, and discrimination. They had been held incommunicado in remote regions of North Korea and subjected to decades of forced labor in mines under such miserable conditions that they often died from exhaustion or starvation. Today it is estimated that only a few hundred of the original 60,000 Korean War POWs remain alive. And yet, they *are* alive, *still* prisoners, *still* wasting away in the North, and *still* yearning to return home.

Unfortunately, the suffering faced by the POWs extends beyond the boundaries of their own lives. In order to tether them to the North and ensure their unending exploitation, the regime encouraged them to get married. Many POWs established families. Like their fathers, the children remained impoverished because of government discrimination. Because they grew up with only limited opportunities, most POW children wound up toiling in the mines alongside their fathers.

In this respect, the story of Mr. Yoo is not unlike that of many other POWs left behind in the North, except for the end. In the beginning, he struggled to survive the difficult labor while avoiding deadly accusations of political crimes. Once he had established a family, he went to extraordinary lengths to provide for them. Yet through it all the government treated him and his family with such casual cruelty and inhumanity that at times he had no choice but to stand by helplessly while his loved ones suffered. Finally, at the age of seventy, after enduring fifty years of oppression and injustice, he took the ultimate leap and embarked upon a journey that could only have one of two outcomes: liberty or death.

"Tears of blood" comes from the Korean expression 피눈물 (*pi-noon-mool*) which describes the agony of watching a loved one suffer. Tears of blood, as we can all understand, result from a pain exceeding anything one might suffer oneself. Mr. Yoo uses the term only once in his autobiography, yet it is thematic of the entire book.

In spite of all the suffering experienced by the POWs during their decades of captivity and all the tears of blood they have shed for loved ones, their plight remains relatively unknown. The Korean War is commonly remembered for military engagements memorialized in black-and-white photos, such as the bloody Chosin Reservoir Campaign or the Battle of Inchon. Contemporary news revolves around crises and provocations, including the infamous shelling of Yeonpyeong Island, November 23, 2010. Amidst all of this, the fading story of 60,000 unreturned South Korean POWs often escapes any mention at all. Their voices remain mute, and their sacrifices are all but forgotten.

It was during the winter break of my sophomore year in high school, 2010-2011, that I first learned about Mr. Yoo's remarkable book. I was vacationing at my grandmother's house in Seoul when my father, who was doing legal research for a non-governmental organization dedicated to helping the South Korean POWs, invited Mrs. Yun-Soon Lee, the daughter of a POW, over for lunch. Mrs. Lee had escaped from North Korea with her father's remains in order to fulfill his final wish, which was to be buried in the South. That day, Mrs. Lee gave me Mr. Yoo's book, whose Korean title was *Starry Nights in Hell*.

After reading Mr. Yoo's autobiography, I felt that it must be translated into English for a worldwide audience so that the story of the Korean War POWs would not be forgotten. The publisher, Won Books, was supportive of my idea, and that is how the project began.

As I went about translating the book, it became clear that there were many topics that an American audience would not understand. As a citizen of the United States, born and raised here, I found certain aspects of Korean history and culture mysterious. I had to research them for myself, which resulted in numerous footnotes throughout the text. Though sources more knowledgeable than I might be able to improve on these explanatory notes, I hope that they will guide Western readers to a fuller understanding of Mr. Yoo's narrative.

The story of the POWs and the plight of the North Koreans is not a matter of history. It remains a serious and ongoing problem. In order to protect the identities of many people referred to in the book, it was necessary to alter or leave out certain names and details.

Finally, Mr. Yoo is a plainspoken man, and his book is the same. It is not a political tract, nor is it particularly artful in construction. But, while it may lack the stylistic gloss of other autobiographies, one cannot help but be awestruck by Mr. Yoo's courage and the simple truthfulness of his testimony. I think that all readers will feel the stunning weight of that simplicity and truthfulness by the time they come to the final scenes of the book. It is not so much what is written in the lines as what is written between them that has such a powerful emotional impact in the end. This is not just a Korean story, or a war story, or an escape story. It is a story of a man who loves his family and simply wants to lead a normal life in the face of endless, needless conflict and suffering. In short, it is a human story.

Paul Taewan Kim
Translator
Mountain View, California
July, 2012

ACKNOWLEDGMENTS

It would have been impossible to translate Mr. Yoo's book alone, and I was fortunate to have the help of many remarkable people. First and foremost among them was the author, Mr. Young-Bok Yoo, whose story of resilience and strength in the face of adversity continues to be an inspiration to me. Others to whom I owe a debt of gratitude include

Mrs. Veronica Oak-Soon Park, the publisher, for giving me, a sixteen-year-old kid, the opportunity to translate the book.

Thomas Yong-Bong Chung, the head of the Korean War POW Affairs – USA in Los Angeles, for all of his encouragement and support.

I would like to add a special thank you to Mr. Yoo, Mrs. Park, and Mr. Chung, who agreed to use all of the proceeds from the book to support the POWs and their families.

David Alzofon, the editor, who took what was essentially an amateur's first draft and made it a real book. He worked with an amazing attention to detail, and asked all of the difficult questions that made it possible for me to put together a book that an American audience could appreciate.

Frankie Frey, the book designer, for her great cover concept and for keeping her cool under considerable deadline pressure.

Also, I would like to thank my family:

My parents, for the infinite support they gave me during the eighteen months it took to finish the project. They spent countless hours helping me read and understand the book, and countless more reviewing my writing, making sure that the translation was accurate. I could not have done this without their help.

And most importantly, my grandmother, Soon-Ja Lee, for teaching me Korean. When I was much younger, she would—in spite of my protests—get me to read Korean books and study the language. It is truly thanks to her that I can speak and read Korean, even though I have never lived in Korea. I am now so grateful that she taught me.

PREFACE

After my return to the South, my life has been one worth living. However, not a moment goes by that I don't think about my siblings and my children, who struggled and starved with me in the North. I also remember my colleagues, the thousands of South Korean POWs. We all suffered the oppression of the North, together.

I cannot help but wonder how thrilled they would be to see what a prosperous and happy nation the South has become. If they could see their fatherland for just one day, they would see that the suffering they went through for the Republic of Korea was not in vain. I know that they would be proud to have served the nation.

To date, seventy-nine South Korean Prisoners of War have succeeded in escaping to the South. Sixteen of those escaped prisoners died after only a few years in the South. I often wonder how many of the prisoners are still alive the North. They must all be around eighty now. Their time is running out. Even now, if only the government would take greater interest in their plight and bring these prisoners home, then they could live out the ends of their lives as free men.

The escaped POWs and their families have established the Family Union of Korean POWs Detained in North Korea, and the Union is collaborating with other international human rights organizations. North Korea still insists that they are not holding any POWs against their will. The Family Union has gathered the testimonies of the escaped POWs to prove that this claim is false. I sincerely hope that the South Korean government will take this problem seriously and bring the POWs home as soon as possible.

Young-Bok Yoo
Seoul
May, 2011

Contact information for the Family Union of Korean POWs Detained in North Korea:

D-633 Yongsan Park, 50-1 Hangang-Ro 1-Ga
Yongsan, Seoul Korea 140-752

Phone: +82-2-976-9982
http://www.kpow.or.kr/
webmaster@kpow.or.kr

MAP OF KOREA

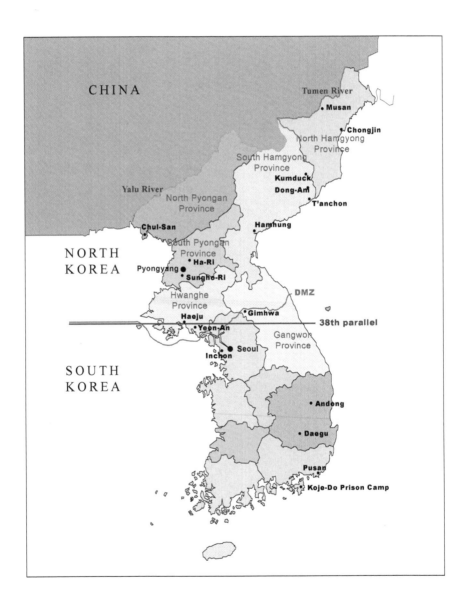

A Country Divided

The map represents Korea as the author knew it as the curtain rises on *Tears of Blood*.

Imperial Japan had occupied the country from 1910 until the end of World War II in 1945. The victorious Allies divided Korea along the 38th parallel, primarily to facilitate an orderly surrender of the Japanese. The North was administered by the Soviet army, answerable to the dictator Joseph Stalin. The South was administered by the American army, under President Harry S. Truman.

As Cold War tensions ramped up, so did hostilities between North and South, whose governments were ideological enemies and sharply disagreed about the arbitrary border division. Still, travel between North and South remained possible.

In July 1948, Syngman Rhee was elected president of South Korea. In September 1948, Communist dictator Kim Il-Sung assumed the office of prime minister of North Korea. War broke out in 1950, when North Korea attacked South Korea, overrunning Seoul and much of South Korea in a lightning campaign that had the tacit approval of the USSR and China.

At the time, the twenty-year-old author was living in Seoul, working during the day and going to night school to make up for lost years under the Japanese occupation and the turmoil of World War II.

In 1953, hostilities ended with a ceasefire. The ceasefire established the Demilitarized Zone (DMZ), a 2.5-mile wide strip of land running across the peninsula that serves as a buffer zone between North and South Korea. The DMZ has stood for almost 60 years as the most heavily militarized border in the world. For the hundreds of thousands of families split by the war, the DMZ is the line that has separated loved ones for decades.

Young-Bok Yoo in 1952, a day before his enlistment in the Republic of Korea Army. With him is his younger sister, Gyung-Eh, who remained in South Korea during the war and greeted him at the airport when he returned home in 2000.

1

The Beginning of a Bleak Future

On Sunday, June 25, 1950, I was hanging out at my friend's boarding room in the Mapo District of Seoul with six of my classmates, waiting for the rain to stop so we could go on a weekend outing. The previous Sunday we had gone hiking, and this weekend we planned to go boating. I had never gone boating with friends before and had been looking forward to the trip all week. At last, it seemed, life was beginning to look up. It was an ordinary day, the kind you might take for granted, but carefree and beautiful in its own way. And yet, five decades would come and go before I was to see another one like it.

All six of us attended the same school, a night school for people holding down day jobs. Although we were all around twenty years old, we were only middle-school students. All of us had missed years of schooling during the Japanese occupation of Korea and the turmoil of World War II. Now we were finally making up for lost time.

Around noon, the skies cleared and the sun came out, so we hopped on a streetcar, and soon we arrived at Mapo Harbor on the north side of the Han River. Seoul has expanded since then and sits on both sides of the river now, but in 1950, the northern riverbank formed the southern border of the city.

Mapo Harbor was a popular hangout, with picnic areas and rowboats for rent. That day, however, it was empty. I was a little surprised. Normally the crowds came here to enjoy the weekend, but there were only a few dock workers who were so preoccupied they didn't seem to notice us.

We looked around. Was it really the weekend? We checked the calendar and it was indeed Sunday. Nobody knew what to do, so we just stood there awhile. Something was wrong; the harbor was just too quiet.

As we idled in place, trying to figure out what was going on, we heard a voice yell, "Hey, you over there!" A newspaperman on a bicycle threw a copy of the day's paper at us. Before we even picked it up, we could see the headline in big black letters: "WAR! NORTH KOREAN ARMY INVADES!"

"At dawn this morning," the article said, "North Korean troops attacked the 38th parallel.[1] They have broken through the defensive lines and are currently en route to Seoul!"

No wonder the dock was deserted. The attack had started early in the morning, so everyone else in the city already knew about it. We simply hadn't heard because we had been inside all day, waiting for dry weather.

"Does this mean there's going to be a war?" one of my friends asked.

"Damn, I don't believe it," said another.

"It says the North Korean Army attacked. How is this not a war?"

"Then what do we do? Should we go farther south? What happens now?"

We weren't sure what was going on. The only thing that was certain was that we weren't going boating that day, so we split up and hurried home.

The next morning, the roads were filled with refugees fleeing southward on foot, so many that it became a human traffic jam. Public transportation was not working, and we could hear the ominous thud of artillery in the distance. In a single day, Seoul had descended into chaos. Of course, no one went to work, and that included my father. He and my

---

[1] Japan occupied Korea from 1910 until the end of World War II. Following the Allied victory over Japan in 1945, the United States and the Soviet Union divided Korea along the 38th parallel, not because the 38th formed a traditional or geographic boundary, but simply because it appeared on most maps. Japanese troops north of the 38th parallel surrendered to the Soviet Union, while the troops south of it surrendered to the United States. In 1948, each army installed Korean-run governments. In the North, the Soviets aided Kim-Il Sung, an exiled guerilla fighter, to become a communist dictator in the mold of Joseph Stalin. Meanwhile, the pro-American South declared statehood, and on July 20, 1948, the popularly elected Constitutional Assembly elected Princeton-educated Syngman Rhee South Korea's first president by an overwhelming majority of 180 out of 196 representatives.

mother spoke quietly about what to do. They dreaded the thought of our family becoming refugees—again.

My father was from Haeju, a port city of about 80,000 people on the coast of the Yellow Sea in what is now North Korea. My mother was from Yeon-An county, a rural farming area only a few miles from Haeju. I was their first child, born on December 20, 1930, when Korea was still a colony of the Japanese Empire.

My father learned carpentry at the Haeju Vocational School. He and my mother were wed in an arranged marriage when he was only fifteen years old.

Although such early marriages were the custom in Korea at the time, my father was not happy at first. He had planned to further his education. But after I was born, his feelings changed, and he became a devoted parent. Soon he had more children. By the time of the war, there were five: me, my sisters Gyung-Eh and Gyung-Sook, and my brothers Young-Nam and Young-Chul—born in that order. My father had little choice but to put aside his plans for school and focus on providing for us. Eventually he found work as a carpentry instructor at Haeju Prison, where he taught the inmates as part of their rehabilitation program.

Perhaps because he had been denied an education, my father believed all the more strongly in it, and instilled this principle in his children. Unfortunately, my education was interrupted, too. I finished elementary school in Haeju, but by then World War II had begun. Japan set about exploiting Korean resources and conscripting students to support its war effort. Life in Korea became very difficult, and I was unable to attend middle school.

On August 15, 1945, when I was fourteen years old, Japan lost World War II, and Korea was liberated. I still remember waving the new Korean flag during the celebration. The Americans and Soviets, who had been allies against Japan, agreed to jointly administer Korea until the Koreans could establish their own independent government. Korea was split in half. The Soviet military was to administer the Peninsula north of the 38th parallel, while the Americans were to administer the south. Haeju, which was just north of the 38th parallel, was under Soviet administration.

When the Soviet forces arrived, we hailed them as liberators, but our happiness was short-lived, as they soon began behaving more like an occupying army, oppressing and exploiting us. After several rapes occurred, women began staying indoors after dark. The Soviet Army

3

also supported the People's Committees, run by local communists. The Committees began to hold investigations of people who were suspected of having been "Japanese collaborators." The "suspects" included just about all government workers, including my father, who was only an employee of the prison. It soon became clear that the investigations were nothing more than a pretext to accuse those who opposed the communists, and fear spread everywhere.

In the midst of this turmoil, my father lost his job. Because of this and the ongoing heat of the investigations, he decided to move the family just a few miles out of town to my mother's home village in Yeon-An County. Though Yeon-An was only a few miles south of Haeju, it was under American administration, so he was safely beyond the reach of the communists.[2]

Unfortunately, there was no carpentry work in Yeon-An, so my father decided to look for work in Seoul, seventy miles to the southeast. Initially he went there alone to get settled. After finding a job at Mapo Prison as a carpentry instructor and acquiring a small place for us to live, he brought us all down from Yeon-An.

Shortly after we moved to Seoul, rival governments were established in Korea: communist in the North, pro-American in the South. The communists began to restrict travel across the 38th parallel into the South, so we could no longer freely go home to Haeju. We had thought that liberation from Japan would be a blessing for all Koreans. Ironically, it led to our introduction to life as a refugee family.

In Seoul, I worked at a roofing tile factory during the day and attended school at night. The Working Students Union also found odd jobs for me, such as peddling goods and delivering newspapers. That was how I managed to earn a living and pay for night school classes. Then, just as things were starting to settle down, the war broke out.

On the second day of the war, we realized we had no choice but to join the mob of refugees fleeing south. We grabbed whatever belongings we could carry and made our way to the Han River,[3] where there was already a massive crowd growing on the riverbank. The only bridge that crossed

---

[2] During a two-year honeymoon period after Korea's liberation from the Japanese, citizens could travel freely between the Soviet-administered north and the American-administered south.

[3] In 1950, when the Han River formed the southern border of the city of Seoul, there was only one bridge from north to south. Alternate bridges crossed the river far to the east, but they were too far away to serve as a detour.

from north to south had already been destroyed, and it was impossible to wade or swim across the river, which was more than half a mile wide. There were a few small boats ferrying people across the river nonstop, but there weren't nearly enough of them to carry all of the refugees across.

We spent the night on the riverbank. Thankfully it was summer, so it wasn't cold. We spent all night trying to find a way across the river, but our efforts were in vain. In the morning the situation only got worse. More people flocked to the riverbank, and we were already exhausted from spending the night outdoors. Furthermore, we had run out of food. With no prospect of getting across the river, there was no longer any reason to stay where we were.

"Dad, let's go back home," I said.

My father agreed, and we made our way through the deluge of people. When we arrived back home, we found refugees from the north squatting at our house. Confirming our worst fears, they told us that North Korean soldiers had already entered Seoul. We were trapped.

That afternoon, I heard loud noises coming from Mapo Prison. In front of the prison, there was a massive North Korean tank flanked by soldiers. One of the soldiers yelled through a megaphone:

"Everyone! Thanks to the Korean People's Army, Seoul has been liberated! Come out, you have nothing to fear!"

The prison doors were flung wide open, and prisoners were being released by the North Korean People's Army. Our world had turned upside down.

In the following days, the North Korean Army of occupation began to assert its influence. They established new agencies to restore order, but just getting food and water was extremely difficult because the markets were closed and nobody was going to work. School, of course, was closed, and there were rumors that students would be drafted into the People's Army. Indeed, recruiting stations were open at every school. At first, enlistment was voluntary, but gradually it became mandatory. We were helpless. Every day was tense and uncertain. I was worried that I would be caught and conscripted into the North Korean Army, so I hid with my friend at his house.

One day while my dad was out trying to find some food, I came home to see my thirteen-year-old sister sitting alone in the house.

"Hey, Gyung-Sook. Come here, I need to talk to you," I said. "If I leave one day and don't come home, it means that they've conscripted me."

She didn't say anything, but she was close to tears.

2

North Korean Soldier

On July 5th, 1950, ten days after the outbreak of war, I was hiding at a friend's house when a group of students barged in. I recognized one of them as an upperclassman at my school. They yelled at us to follow them back to the school, or else. We were afraid, but we had no choice—we had to go with them.

There were already many other students in the schoolyard, as well as a few fully armed North Korean regular soldiers. I realized I was walking right into a conscription center. My heart skipped a beat. When my friend and I hesitated at the school entrance, the older boys shoved us forward.

"What are you guys doing? Hurry up! Let's go!" they yelled.

"But...."

"What's the matter? You're going to enlist, aren't you?"

I realized that these upperclassmen were communist sympathizers. There were many students like them who welcomed the North Korean Army and pressured their classmates into enlisting for the North. At first they tried to persuade students to join of their own accord, but persuasion gradually became forced conscription. I had done my best to avoid them by staying away from the school and home, but they had finally caught me.

I carefully tried to talk my way out of this predicament. "Please, sir, could I quickly swing by my house?" I asked politely.

He made a face. "You're going to try to escape, aren't you!" he yelled angrily.

I quickly replied, "No, sir, not at all."

"Then enlist right now!" he demanded.

"Please, let me think about it," I begged.

"What's there to think about! It is an honor to be given the opportunity to fight for the liberation of our nation. What could you possibly need to think about?"

I sensed that if I hesitated any longer I'd be dragged off by force. My friend was flustered. I tried to get away again, this time using more tact.

"Would it be all right if I let my parents know first?" I asked.

"You're not getting counterrevolutionary feelings are you?" they asked.

"No, no—of course not."

"Then listen closely." He lowered his voice threateningly and said, "The North is definitely gonna win this war, so you're gonna have to serve in the army at some point, if not today. If you try to escape, you'll get your family in trouble too. Do you want to see your family go to prison?"

As he said this, his cronies surrounded us to make sure we couldn't get away.

Just then, one of the officers called out to us.

"What's goin' on?" he yelled.

"Sir," the senior crisply saluted the officer, "We're on our way to enlist!"

"You are impressive students. Move along."

The senior took my hand and dragged us into the schoolyard. With the North Korean officer keeping a close eye on us, there was no way for me to escape. Even if I did get away, I knew they would find me again, and my family would be in danger as well. I resigned myself to my fate.

There were many other nervous-looking students at the "recruitment" center, all caught between a rock and a hard place, all wearing the same worried expression. My friend and I got in the enlistment line.

"Name?" the recruitment officer asked.

"Young-Bok Yoo."

"School?"

"Soong-Mun middle school."

"Are you healthy?"

"I guess."

And just like that, I became a soldier in the Korean People's Army (KPA), the official name of the North Korean Army.

The new conscripts were taken to a former U.S. Army base and were issued uniforms. As I put on my uniform, I felt that I was slowly losing control of my own life. I was being forced into a difficult and hopeless world.

We then spent a few days doing some basic training at the base, where they taught us how to operate a machine gun, shoot rifles, and throw grenades. Then an officer came and picked out thirty of us to go with him to the front. We boarded a train south, but due to American bombing, the train was slow and had to stop often. When we arrived at Wonju, ninety miles southeast of Seoul, we had to get off the train because the tracks ahead had been destroyed.

Though we were wearing North Korean soldiers' uniforms, we were not issued any weapons. We were told we would be given guns once we joined with the main army.

We traversed the countryside, walking all day on country roads. Every time we walked through a village, all the townsfolk came out and watched us with sympathetic expressions—all the townsfolk, that is, except the young men, who were conspicuously missing.[4]

One of the other soldiers in my unit was a friend and classmate of mine, Guk-Joo Jung. During our march, he told us we were near his hometown. He hoped that we would pass through there, since he might see his family. Luckily for him, we did indeed pass through his hometown.

As usual, all the villagers were out watching us march by. Guk-Joo anxiously scanned the crowd for someone he recognized. Then he saw his mother.

---

[4] Most young men had probably gone into hiding or run away from the North Korean press-gangers.

"Guk-Joo!" she cried.

"Mother!"

They had a moving reunion. Our officer gave us permission to stop so that Guk-Joo could spend some time with his mom. The villagers all gave us some food, and we got a brief respite. But before we knew it, the break was over. As we left, Guk-Joo's mother said to him through her tears, "You must come back safe. Make sure to stay safe…" Tears were flowing down Guk-Joo's face as he turned away from her. After we had walked pretty far down the road, I looked back and saw Guk-Joo's mother, still standing in the same place we had left her.

A few days later, we joined with the main army. I was reassigned to the KPA, 101st Pacification Regiment, 11th Battalion, 45th Company, 1st Platoon. This regiment, made up mostly of student enlistees, was to follow behind the main force and mop up any remnants of the enemy hiding out in the countryside. As the North Korean Army quickly advanced south, small groups of South Korean soldiers often hid in the brush and let the main army pass by. Later, they would ambush small units like ours. This caused our unit to suffer heavier casualties than the main army.

It was a hellish march. The road was often cut off because of the bombing, which not only slowed us down but also made getting supplies more difficult. Exhausted, we marched day and night, while sustaining heavy casualties due to the rough terrain and combat.

Whenever a firefight broke out, we were highly vulnerable. During one fierce battle, Guk-Joo was killed. We were too busy to bury him properly. The best we could do was cover his body with a few branches.

My throat went dry when I remembered his mother's weeping face as she begged him to come back safely. I had seen many people die since the march started, but when Guk-Joo was killed, I was unable to get over it. Fear and anxiety filled my thoughts for days. *How many other young students' precious lives had already been wasted? How many more would die? Would I ever make it out safely?*

The tragedy and sorrow of war haunted me every waking moment, and I wondered constantly if I would ever see my family again. Did they know what kind of trouble I was in? If I died like Guk-Joo, would my mother ever know what had happened to me? Would anyone? The thought of my mother and the desire to see her again drove me to survive and make it home.

3

My First Escape

In September, 1950, a little over two months after I had been press-ganged into the KPA, a soldier found a propaganda leaflet on the side of the road saying that UN forces had landed at Inchon, near Seoul.[5] At first we didn't believe it, but on the other hand, our advance had stalled, and we weren't getting any supplies from the rear.

The officers didn't tell us anything, but the mood among the troops was grim. It was in this atmosphere that our entire battalion was ordered to assemble at a field near a small river, where we were addressed by a high-ranking officer.

"This army has been ordered to advance," he said. "Be prepared for heavy combat. Also, we need to move quickly, so all injured or ill soldiers shall be separated," he added. "If you are ill or injured, step forward now."

Should I go with the main unit, or should I pretend to be sick? I wasn't sure what would happen to the soldiers who stepped forward. Would they be executed? Either way, I had to make up my mind fast. I decided to take a gamble; I didn't want to be dragged along like this anymore. With my fate hanging in the balance, I stepped forward.

From there, everything happened quickly. After the unfit for combat were separated, the main force packed up and set off immediately, leaving

---

[5] Inchon is a port city on the Yellow Sea, just south of the 38th parallel and thirty miles west of Seoul. The Inchon landing was a turning point in the Korean War. Today, Inchon International Airport is South Korea's main airport.

a few dozen of the injured and weak soldiers behind under the command of one minor officer. We slowly followed in the rear, and soon we had drifted far behind the main regiment.

The officer walked far ahead of us, allowing the stragglers to march along at their own pace. We became spread out, with the injured lagging far behind the fit. I walked with three other student enlistees. Once the four of us were alone, we spoke quietly to one another. It turned out that they wanted to escape, too, and we decided to get away at the first opportunity.

The escape itself was simple. We arrived at a crossroads, and when no one was watching, we simply went a different direction from the main group. For weeks I had not dared to entertain the thought of freedom, but now, I was free. It was almost too easy.

The four of us walked several miles on a country trail. We were looking for a village where we could collect our bearings and find a way home.

"Put your hands up!"

A voice rang out from the side of the road, and we were immediately surrounded by South Korean soldiers brandishing their guns at us. We ourselves were unarmed.

"Don't shoot! We're only students! We were forced to join the North Korean Army. We escaped and we just wanna go home!"

One of the soldiers laughed at us. "You idiots! Do you think we give a shit if you're students or not? If you're wearing a North Korean uniform, then as far as we're concerned, you're one of the bastards who's been trying to kill us."

There was nothing we could do. We were prisoners of the South Korean Army. The soldiers took us to a small town where other captured North Korean soldiers were being held, many of them student enlistees. An officer began to question us. We tried to explain to him that we had been forced into the army, but he didn't care.

"If you spent a single day fighting for the North Korean Army, you are our enemy. Whatever the circumstances, you guys fought against us, didn't you?"

There was nothing we could say. He was right; it was true that we had fought against South Korean troops.

"What's your name?"

"Where do you live?"

"What school do you go to?"

"Who lives with you?"

They quickly interrogated us and threw us into Andong[6] Jail, where American soldiers were detaining prisoners of war. I had thought the South Korean soldiers were on my side, I had thought they would rescue us—but to them, a North Korean soldier was a North Korean soldier. It was so unfair! All sorts of thoughts crossed my mind. I even half-wondered if it would have been better just to stay with the main army. At least then I wouldn't have been a prisoner.

The next day we were taken to a larger prisoner-of-war camp near Pusan, the biggest port in Korea, on the southeast tip of the Peninsula. The camp was a huge field covered in massive tents. At this camp, we were told to wear a uniform with the letters "P.W." on the back, and a necklace with a unique identification number. I found out that P.W. meant "prisoner of war."

Soldiers were stationed on guard duty, but they did not interrogate us, nor were we allowed to ask them questions about the war or about our future. In fact, the guards completely ignored us when we asked them questions. I was treated less like a person and more like a number.

When I defected from the North Korean Army, I just wanted to go home. Now they're branding me as just another prisoner of war, like any North Korean soldier—it's ridiculous! It was a thought that kept recurring to me, but no matter how many times I went over it, there was simply nothing I could have done to avoid this fate. I worried about my future and my family, too. *Are they still alive? Do they know that I'm a prisoner?*

Life in the camp was miserable. There were fifty of us to each tent. The ground was soggy and wet, and the tents did little to protect us from the weather. The American Army gave each prisoner just two blankets, a raincoat, and a bowl for food. They fed us old rice and watery soup, and we were given so little food that we were constantly hungry, even right after we ate.

We spent most of our day setting up tents for the new prisoners. When winter set in, camp life got worse. Our thin blankets could not protect us

---

[6] Andong is a town located in the southeastern corner of South Korea.

from the cold. I spent many miserable nights curled up in a ball, trying to stay warm.

Finally spring came. Better weather improved our physical condition, but we still had no idea what was happening outside the walls of the camp. Judging by the steady stream of new prisoners, the war was still raging.

One day we were all told to pack up our belongings and follow the American soldiers to the docks. We were being transferred. After a long boat trip, we arrived at the Koje-Do POW Camp.[7] As soon as we landed, we had to pitch our tents and make our own living spaces.

In our sector alone, there were four to five thousand captured soldiers. I later learned that over 170,000 soldiers had been interned at Koje-Do— the population of a large city. As prisoners, we all had the same questions on our minds: *What would happen to us? When was the war going to end?*

---

[7] Koje-Do, the second largest island in South Korea, lies off the southern coast.

4

Koje-Do Prisoner-of-War Camp

At Koje-Do we followed a strict daily routine. When we woke up, we would roll up our tent walls first so that the guards could see inside. Then, as long as it didn't rain or snow, we were forced to do various types of labor. The hardest job was to transport rocks and boulders to a crusher. The crushed stone was used to make gravel, which the military needed to build new roads.

The camp conditions were atrocious. We drank poorly purified river water that often got us sick. There were no showers, and after a long day we would be coated in a layer of sweat and dust we could not wash off. Fleas crawled all over our hair and our clothes. We were so covered in fleas that instead of catching them one by one, we just tried to shake them off. Over time, this chronic griminess caused many of us to develop rashes and skin diseases. To fight the skin-disease epidemic, the Army sprayed DDT all over our tents and our beds before we slept. They hoped the DDT would kill some of the insect pests, but it also made our rashes worse.

Hunger was a constant issue. Since we were never given enough to eat, we would steal extra food whenever we could. The prisoners whose job was to unload bags of rice onto the island were especially lucky, since they had many opportunities to steal some of the cargo. Even a small handful of extra rice was cause for joy. Of course, there were harsh punishments for those who got caught, but a little extra food was incentive enough to drive many prisoners to steal.

Eventually vendors began setting up shop just outside the prison, hoping to trade food for the prisoners' belongings. The blankets, raincoats, boots, and clothing that we received from the UN were considered high quality. Every time we were given fresh sets of clothes, boots, or raincoats, many prisoners would trade their new gear for food, while they kept on using their old gear. This was against the rules, but by bartering for sweets and delicious dried fish, many prisoners found a little comfort and hope in the hellish prison camp.

The prisoners gradually divided themselves into different factions based on their various military allegiances: North Korean regulars, Chinese soldiers, and student enlistees. Though some—especially the regulars—staunchly maintained their communist identity, most student enlistees did not consider themselves communist, and in my area of the prison, we actively rejected the label. Once, we were given clothes dyed blood red, indicating we were communists, but we refused to wear them and hung them up against the fence instead. We were never given red clothing again.

Prisoner re-education programs were common in the camps. We were given propaganda leaflets made by the U.S. Army that contained information revealing the atrocities committed by the Communist forces and telling of the impending American victory.

The pamphlets also focused a great deal on the illegitimacy of Kim Il-Sung as a leader. They claimed that he was nothing more than a puppet ruler put in place as a result of the sinister collaboration between Mao Zedong and Joseph Stalin, and they accused the immature Kim of starting a tragic war that had wreaked havoc on the lives of the Korean people.

These propaganda pamphlets were meant to convert the prisoners to the South Korean cause, but they were often an opportunity for hardcore communists to affirm their beliefs by denying that the pamphlets were true. These pamphlets deepened the rift between prisoners of different ideologies. Arguments and fights were common between the hardcore communists and the so-called "anti-communist POWs." Most prisoners did not want to get involved in these fights, so they kept their ideologies to themselves.

A few months into my incarceration, a virus began to go around the camps, and doctors were brought in to treat us. To my surprise, I recognized one of them. He was the head physician of the hospital that I used to go to when I lived in Seoul.

16

I was overjoyed to see someone I knew. "You're the head physician at Bak-Ae Hospital in Seoul, right?" I asked him.

"Yeah, I am," he replied, surprised. "Do I know you?"

"I lived in the government homes across the street from the hospital. I've been there a few times."

"Oh, really? Yeah, you do look familiar," he said in a kindly tone.

We had a short conversation, during which he encouraged me to hang in there because the war was going to be over soon. I gave him my family's address and asked him to contact them for me when he went back to Seoul, but he told me that unfortunately he had already moved to Pusan to avoid the fighting. He also said that amidst the chaos of war it was unlikely that my family was still living there.

"It's not much," he said, "but I want you to have this." He handed me some money, and then left. His gift was enormously helpful. I hoped to meet him again sometime after I was freed and thank him for his kindness. It was the first time I had spoken to someone from outside the camp since my capture.

I wondered what was going to happen to the prisoners when the war ended. This question was on the minds of all the POWs. Some said that one and all would be sent back to North Korea, while others believed we would be allowed to choose which side to go to. If I had a choice, I thought, I would definitely go to the South. I had family living there, I had no communist beliefs, and I had been forced into a North Korean uniform.

In June, 1952, after I had spent a little more than a year at Koje-Do—and two years in all as a POW—the prison officials released a statement saying that the student enlistees would be screened with regard to their repatriation. Though there were no guarantees, those who had been press-ganged into the military hoped that a "screening" meant that we would be given a choice as to which side we would be repatriated.

At first, I was sure that if I had a choice, I would return to the South. However, some prisoners pointed out that the South would not accept us because we had fought for the North. Instead, they argued that we should go to the North, because only in the North would be welcome. The argument did make sense, so I was unsure of the best option. I was also afraid that if I returned to the South, I would subject my family to discrimination. However, I did not hesitate for long. Going to North Korea would

17

mean a permanent separation from my family, and I could never allow that to happen. I decided to return to the South no matter what.

Finally, the screening day came. There was a tense atmosphere in the prison. Here and there, small groups of prisoners speculated about it. Other prisoners were silently staring off into the distance. After breakfast, a large tent was set up outside the prison, and several screening officials sat under the canopy. The officials wore military uniforms, but they didn't have any ribbons or medals, so I assumed that they were civilians.

In the end, the screening process was very straightforward. When it was my turn, the officer asked me, "Do you want to be repatriated to the North, or do you want to stay here in the South?"

"I want to go home to Seoul, so that I can see my family and go back to school," I said.

The officer just nodded and told me to go to one of the tents for prisoners who wanted to stay in the South. After all that anxiety, the simplicity of the process was almost a letdown.

That afternoon, after all the prisoners had made their decisions, I was a little surprised to find that quite a few student enlistees had chosen to be repatriated to the North. Only a few days ago these students had said that they were going to remain in the South. I couldn't understand why they had changed their minds. Maybe they feared living with the label of a being a former North Korean soldier. Either way, I wonder now if they came to regret that decision.

Later that afternoon, the prisoners who chose to stay in the South were transported back to the mainland and set free. While I waited to be released, I decided that I would rather die than fight for the North again. My eyes suddenly watered as I thought about my ordeal as a soldier and my time in the POW camp. I thought of my family, too and how we would all be reunited again soon. Sadly, though, these hopes were soon to become just another casualty of war.

5

Reunion

When faced with hardship, some people just give up and accept their fate, while others go to extraordinary lengths to change their destiny. The lucky ones succeed in making a small difference. When the war turned my life upside down twice, I always tried to get back the life I had lost. I could only do this because of my great desire to see my family. I wasn't alone in this. Despite being locked up like animals, many POWs endured the suffering for months, if not years, in hopes of seeing their families again.

The prisoners were released in June of 1952 and transferred to the mainland. There we were finally able to take off the P.W. shirts that we had worn for two years. It was not until I changed into civilian clothes that I truly felt free. I cried for a long time, with my face buried in my new clothes.

We were taken to Suwon, a small city south of Seoul, where a huge crowd of people welcomed us. Some of the ladies handed out rice balls to us. When I took a bite, the rice tasted like honey. They also comforted us, saying it would all be okay. I was overwhelmed by this warm welcome. On the one hand, I was grateful for their generosity, but on the other, I felt guilty because I had fought for the North.

At Suwon, the government gave me a free transportation pass. They also gave me a month's rations—46 pounds of rice and a few cans of food—and let me keep the blankets I had used in Koje-Do.

As I crossed the Han River from south to north on the rebuilt bridge, I set foot in Seoul for the first time in two years. First, I went to the tile factory where I used to work, in hopes of getting information about my family's location. I didn't think that going to Mapo Prison would help, since it was doubtful that anyone who knew my father would still be working there. I met the owner of the factory, but he was not sure where my family had gone. He had heard that some people who worked at Mapo Prison had taken their families to Daegu[8] to escape the war.

I rushed back across the Han River to Daegu as quickly as I could. When I arrived, I asked people if they knew where the Mapo Prison employees were staying. My search finally brought me to a large building where I found a woman standing inside, near the entrance. I asked if she knew my father, but she didn't recognize his name, so I asked if she knew a girl named "Gyung-Eh."

"Oh, Gyung-Eh? How do you know her?"

"I'm her brother."

"Oh, you are? Come with me!"

She quickly went inside and spread the word to find Gyung-Eh. After a few minutes, another woman came toward us with a young lady I immediately recognized as my sister. She came running toward me and we had a tearful reunion.

"Where have you been? We have all been so worried about you!"

Amidst the tears, I could not properly respond. Instead I asked her about our family. Luckily everyone was fine. My father had gone to Seoul for some business only a few days ago, and my mother had taken my other sister, Gyung-Sook, and my brothers, Young-Nam and Young-Chul, to my mother's hometown in Yeon-An County, near Haeju. Yeon-An was a rural area, and they hoped it would be a haven from the fighting.

I was also surprised to learn that during the turmoil of the war, my parents had had another child; I now had a third sister named Myung-Sook. She, too, was in Yeon-An with my mother. I wanted to see my mother and my new sister as soon as possible, but I had responsibilities that came first. I had to return to Seoul to work and help my father make a living.

---

[8] Daegu, now a major transportation hub and a commercial center, is about 150 miles south of Seoul. At the time of the Korean War, it was a smaller city, best known for its delicious apples.

My sister asked me again what had happened to me, and though I wanted to tell her, I did not want to reveal that I had fought for the North in front of all the other people watching our reunion. I avoided her questions for the rest of the day, and then the next morning I set off for Seoul again to see my father. This time I went straight to the Mapo Prison, where I found him and went through another tearful reunion.

"You rascal, where have you been? There hasn't been any news about you—what could you have been doing? I thought that you had died! But you're fine. Thank god you're safe..."

Then my dad choked up and could not continue. All I could say was, "I'm really sorry, father. I'm really sorry."

Over the two years we'd been separated by the war, my father had grown so thin that it was hard to recognize him. The worry lines etched on his face testified to the unspeakable struggles he had been through. I could only imagine how difficult it must have been for him to evacuate my mother and siblings from Seoul, care for my sister, Gyung-Eh, and lose me, all at the same time.

I told him that I had met Gyung-Eh, but again I could not bring myself to reveal the true story of my time in Koje-Do. I just told him that the press-gangers had found me at my friend's house. With a look of understanding, my father did not ask me any more questions.

Thanks to his job at Mapo Prison, my father was able to acquire a small house in Seoul, and when we brought Gyung-Eh back from Daegu we were able to feel like a family again. My father decided that he would fetch my mother and the rest of my brothers and sisters from Yeon-An once we were completely settled in Seoul.

Though life had returned to normal, I didn't feel normal. While I felt blessed to be alive and with my family again, the memories of Koje-Do Prison and Guk-Joo's death weighed heavily on me. I told myself that I could survive anything after what I had been through. I also promised myself to visit Guk-Joo's parents one day, and tell them how their beloved son had died. I did not know at the time that this would be a promise I could never keep.

6

ROK

Though I had hoped to rest awhile after my time in Koje-Do and maybe resume my studies at school, the war still wasn't over, and a month after we settled down in Seoul, I received a draft order from the South Korean military. With other young soldiers sacrificing their lives for the cause, I knew that I had to give up my own interests. It was also an opportunity to make amends for the time I'd spent fighting for the North.

"You've only been back a few weeks, and already you're going to leave again," my father sighed. However, he also knew that fighting for the South would help me redeem myself. Deep down I had always known that I would join the South Korea Army in the war effort, but somehow I had not expected to be called to arms so soon.

I sat down and wrote a letter to my sister:

Gyung-Eh,

I'm sorry that I have to leave so soon, but please, I don't want you to feel sorry for me. Whatever happens, I hope you realize that this is the best way for me to make up for my time as a North Korean soldier. Being a South Korean soldier is also something for me to be proud of. I promise that I will fight hard and return home safely. While I'm gone, take care of father, and if I don't come back, be strong for me and remember that countless others have also given up their lives for their country in this war...

I realized that this letter might well be my last words to my family, and I began to add things I wanted to say to my mother and brothers and sisters as well. The letter ended up being ten pages long. I made sure to leave nothing out. Even as I reassured my mother that there was nothing to worry about, the thought that I might not return would overpower me at times, and I had to pause to steady myself and hold back the tears.

Two days later, I was on the platform at Seoul Station saying goodbye to my dad and my sister. It was only a few moments before my train departed for the army camps. As I heaved my things onboard, my dad called out to me one last time.

"I know that you will fulfill your duty to your country honorably, son. I have faith in you. And always remember that we are waiting for you. Once you come home, our family will be together again. Don't lose hope!"

Holding back the tears, I managed to force a grin, and with that, the train departed from the station.

The train took us to the Nonsan military training center, about ninety miles south of Seoul. There, we got our uniforms. It felt strange to be putting on the Republic of Korea (ROK)[9] Army uniform, since only two years ago this had been the uniform of the enemy.

At the Nonsan boot camp, we spent about a month in basic training. The training was rigorous and thorough, since unlike the KPA, the ROK Army sincerely tried to make us into effective soldiers. But in comparison to the Koje-Do Prison Camp, the training was a piece of cake. Once one has gone through serious hardship, any smaller challenges that might come after that are easy.

After training, we were sent to the forward command base in Gangwon Province, near the 38th parallel, to receive our troop assignments. Many soldiers were afraid of the fighting and hoped to be assigned to the rear. I was scared too, but I wanted to be at the front so that I could fight valiantly and wash away my sin of fighting for the communists.

In August, 1952, I was assigned to the 5th Division, 27th Regiment. At Division headquarters I was put aboard a truck and sent from there to the 3rd Battalion, 3rd Company, 1st Platoon, on the front line. My platoon sat entrenched on a lonely, nameless hill somewhere in the Gimhwa region of Gangwon Province. Directly in front of us was the ominously quiet enemy

---

[9] The Republic of Korea Army (ROK) is the official name of the South Korean Army.

territory. Though at times it seemed deserted, every once in a while there were fierce firefights. We were on guard at all times.

According to the senior officers, there was a peace process going on behind the scenes. If there was a ceasefire, the borders would be drawn along the current battle lines. Ironically, this drove constant fighting. Both sides fought harder to win a little more territory just before the ceasefire, and we were told that the enemy would launch a major offensive soon.

After a while, I got used to life on the front line. There was always the threat of battle looming over our heads, but whenever I looked at the scores of tanks deployed behind us, I felt safe. Though there was not much fighting, there were scouting missions that took us right up to the enemy lines. My buddies would try to avoid going on these missions, but I would always volunteer because I had something to prove. I felt like I had to make up for the time I had fought for the North. The corporals and sergeants trusted me to get things done.

On June 9, 1953, roughly a year after I had enlisted, I was assigned to an overnight scouting detail. My unit descended into the valley below and dug in for the night. As darkness fell, we could hear artillery and gunfire in the nearby hills; it seemed as if the fighting was fiercer that night than ever before. We spent the night wide awake and alert, listening carefully for the slightest sound. I had a dreadful feeling that we would be attacked.

But nothing happened all night, and by the next morning we had begun to relax and feel drowsy. A few soldiers got out of the foxholes and stretched out. It felt nice to release the tension from the previous night.

Suddenly we heard artillery thundering nearby. It was the type of barrage that always came before an infantry charge. *We were going to be attacked!* Adrenaline pumping, we grabbed our weapons and looked for the enemy.

The artillery began to land closer and closer to our position. Dirt and dust filled the air as we tried to take cover. Through the smoke, we began to make out enemy soldiers flooding into the valley. There were so many of them! It was the Chinese Army, using their notorious human-wave attack. A staggering number of soldiers charged us.

We yelled into the radio "It's the Chinese! There's tons of them!" It was the last transmission we sent.

Chaos ensued. There was no hope of retreat. All we could do was try to hold our ground against the onslaught. We frantically fired our weapons at anything that moved, while artillery shells began raining down directly on top of our position. The sound of Chinese bugles drowned out the gunfire. Explosions were going off all around us, and I could hear people yelling. Then everything went white.

When I came to, I found that my foxhole had collapsed, burying the lower half of my body in debris. I couldn't move. There were Chinese soldiers everywhere, and all my buddies were dead. A wave of fear surged through me like electricity.

The battle was over. The Chinese soldiers began treating the wounded and collecting their dead. I closed my eyes and tried to play dead. Then a soldier came up close to me, and instinctively I reached for my gun. He heard my movement and immediately called out to the other Chinese soldiers. I had been discovered.

7

Captured

"I'm done for, I'm dead," I thought. I was caught between the jaws of death with no way out. I remembered my friend Guk-Joo. *Did his parents know that he had died? Would my parents know how I died?* My heart pumped hard, rebelliously, as if it knew it had only a little time left and was desperately trying to pound out a lifetime of beats.

I waited for death, but no bullet came. Instead, the Chinese soldiers began to dig me out from the caved-in foxhole. They managed to pull me out in a few minutes, but I couldn't move because the blood to my legs had been cut off for so long. They tried to make me stand, but I couldn't, so they lifted me up and carried me back to their camp.

At the camp, I was taken to a field hospital where a Chinese nurse came and attended to my injuries. Thankfully, I had not been hurt badly, and after a short while I was able to move the lower half of my body again.

Once I recovered, a translator came and asked for my name, rank, and serial number, and then about some other personal details. It had been just a year since my release from Koje-Do, and I was a POW again, this time of the Chinese Communists. The grim reality of my situation began to sink in, but at least this was better than dying in the dirt. Later I found out that I had been captured less than two months before the ceasefire. I was twenty-three years old, and another difficult chapter of my life was just beginning.

I spent a few more days in the field hospital. When I had recovered enough, I was taken to a building in a nearby town that was serving as a makeshift hospital, where Chinese medics treated both wounded South Korean POWs and Chinese soldiers. I was surprised that the Chinese doctors treated the POWs and the soldiers equally, just as they had in the field hospital.

While I was being held, there were several air strikes on the town. Though there was a Red Cross emblem above the building and even a "P.W." sign, the planes continued to bomb, perhaps because they thought the signs and the emblem were only camouflage. One day the hospital was hit, and part of it collapsed. I saw many Chinese medics risk their lives carrying the wounded on their backs to a safer place. They even saved us POWs. There was gunfire and explosions, but the medical staff braved the danger. I was impressed by their sense of duty and responsibility.

After a few more weeks of treatment, I was able to walk on my own again. I was cleared from the hospital and taken to the Sungho-Ri POW Camp in the South Pyongan Province, near the North Korean capital of Pyongyang. This POW camp was run by the North Korean Army. We were processed there and divided into groups, just as we had been at Koje-Do.

Then one day we saw fireworks to the north, in Pyongyang. We learned that the ceasefire had been signed.[10] It was shocking news. Though we knew that peace negotiations had been in progress, we were not sure they would ever succeed. Now the war was finally over. Loud cheers spread around the camp. Now that there was peace, there would probably be a prisoner exchange soon, and I would be free again. Or so I thought.

"What's going to happen to us?" I asked one of the guards cautiously.

"You will be dealt with according to international law," he said.

This was just an automatic response. We thought that he responded like this because the issue was above his pay grade.

However, after a few days, there were no changes to the camp. If they were going to exchange prisoners, like they had done at Koje-Do Prison, the officials should be asking us whether we wanted to go back to South Korea or stay in the North. Instead, the rules got a little stricter, and we were put under closer surveillance.

---

[10] The Korean War Armistice Agreement was signed on July 27, 1953. No peace treaty has ever been signed; the two nations are still officially in a state of war.

A few days later, an order came to pack up our things and prepare to march. I felt that something was amiss. We walked all day and arrived at a small town called Ha-Ri, in South Pyongan Province.

As soon as we arrived, we had to set up our tents, just like at Koje-Do. Then, on the second day, the prisoner re-education program began. The re-education was mostly about the superiority of North Korea and the leadership of the "Hero of Heroes" Kim-Il Sung. It was all just political indoctrination. To a bunch of prisoners desperate to go home, their words fell upon deaf ears. They gave us paper and told us to write a journal about our lives, from birth up to the present. We were worried. Why were they making us do this weird stuff? Shouldn't they be getting ready to send us home? Some of us remained hopeful and could not imagine why the North Koreans would keep us now that the war was over.

The indoctrination continued for two months. During that time, they made us write our autobiography over and over again. The prisoners paid close attention to what was going on as we tried to figure out their motives and what it all might mean for our future. But whatever their plans were for us, the officials weren't saying. Instead they told us that Korean reunification was imminent, and if we studied hard we could become leaders in the new communist Korean society. Not many of us believed them.

8

Exile

The ceasefire had been signed, but instead of being repatriated, the POWs were transferred again. This time we were taken farther north, to Chul-San, a mining town in North Pyongan Province. On the way there, we passed through the war-torn countryside. Looking at the ruined fields and destroyed villages, one could not fail to sense the destructiveness, the futility of war. Finally we came to what seemed like dormitories for miners. No sooner had we arrived than they forced us to start mining with old, primitive hand tools. We were getting anxious. What did they have planned for us?

At the Chul-San Mine, we were mining for *monazite*, a mineral that was found under flat ground mixed with sand.[11] We were told that the mineral was being exported to the USSR for use in weapons-grade steel.[12] To mine it, we first used explosives to blast through the top layer of soil. Once we dug holes about four to five meters deep, we extracted the sand, which had to be filtered to leave only the monazite. Finally, the pure monazite sand was packaged into 50-kilogram boxes and shipped off. Mining monazite was backbreaking work, and dangerous, too, since we weren't given proper equipment or tools. Some POWs were even killed

---

[11] Monazite is a reddish-brown phosphate mineral that is rich in the rare earth metals.

[12] In reality, monazite, which contains significant amounts of the radioactive element thorium, was used by the USSR in nuclear weapons research.

during the blasting. On top of all this work, we had to attend political re-education classes several times a week.

In the beginning of October, relocation orders were given once again, and we packed all of our belongings and boarded a freight car. I didn't know where we were going exactly, but judging by the steep mountains, I guessed that we were heading north again.

After several days, my suspicions were confirmed when we passed the Ryong-Yang Mine, in South Hamgyong Province. We were now in the cold and mountainous Northeast.[13] Finally, on October 8, 1954, we got off the train at the Kumduck Mine. It was a large mine with a small village for the workers. We put our stuff down in what used to be a cultural center.

One of the officers addressed us. "Make yourselves comfortable. For now, this is where you will spend the night," he said. "You will stay here until you finish building your barracks."

If we were building barracks, did that mean we would be staying here for a while? What about prisoner repatriation? I was filled with misgivings about the whole situation. However, survival was more important at the moment, so I did as I was told.

Our barracks were built upstream of a large river that flowed through the mountains. It was very high up, around 600 meters, so the nights and mornings were freezing cold. We had to scavenge for building materials in the nearby hills—wood for the walls and dried reeds from the field for the roof. We worked almost nonstop to get our shelter built before winter set in. Once we finished building our quarters, they sent us to work in the mines.

There were also some changes to our identification. We were no longer referred to as POWs, but were called the "1708th Interior Ministry Construction Brigade," and given regular Army uniforms. We also got a commanding officer, Colonel In-Ho Jo, his staff of officers, about sixty guards, and a few medics. They erased our status as POWs and turned us into miners deep in the North. Home felt like it was getting farther and farther away.

---

[13] Winters in South Hamgyong Province can reach lows of -35° Fahrenheit.

9

The Politics of Mining

The first official duty of the 1708th Construction Brigade was to shovel muddy ore into 80-kilogram bags, carry each bag on our backs, and load them into trucks. It was utterly exhausting labor. Each of us had a quota of bags that we had to fill and load every day. If we failed to meet the quota, we were threatened with closer monitoring and intimidated by some of the officers. If we did a good job by bringing in more than our quota, all we got was our name on a wall and a pat on the back.

Even Koje-Do Prison had not been this bad. Sure, life was tough there, too, but this hard labor was unbearable. After carrying a massive bag on my back all day, it felt like my spine was going to snap. The conditions we lived under went completely against international standards for the treatment of prisoners of war.

Soon we were sent to work in the mines themselves. We were given all the hard jobs, such as pushing the minecarts around and drilling holes in the rock for explosives. The mineshafts wound for over fifteen kilometers and burrowed up to three kilometers deep underground, where it was pitch black and the air reeked of explosive fumes left over from the blasting. It was dangerous and toxic. There was a chance of a cave-in after every explosion, and dust filled the air and damaged our lungs. But there was no adequate treatment if you got hurt or sick, so if you were hurt even once, it was almost impossible to get better. We were treated like trash; we were expendable.

Kumduck Mine is the oldest, biggest mine in North Korea, producing zinc, copper, and other metals. It is one of North Korea's most important natural resources. Mining even continued during the Korean War. Since the mining had gone on nonstop since the Japanese occupation, all the easy ore had been extracted. To get to the ore now, we had to extend the tunnels, and every day they got longer and deeper.

Soon our group was joined by the 1707th Construction Brigade, which was also made up of POWs. Together, there were about a thousand South Korean POWs being exploited for slave labor in the Kumduck region. Some were sent to smaller mines nearby, others laid new railroad track, which was especially dangerous, since a lot of blasting had to be done in order to level the ground. We were forced to work in three eight-hour shifts, round-the-clock. We could focus only on day-to-day survival. We didn't have the time or the energy to think about our future.

Why did the North Koreans never return the POWs to the South? Perhaps it was because after the war, much of Korea was in ruins. There was a lot of construction to do and not enough young men to do it after so many had died in combat. Tens of thousands of captured South Korean soldiers were a perfect solution—we could be exploited at no cost.

We were also forced to attend re-education classes at Kumduck. The instructors tried to brainwash us, saying that we had to be loyal to the Korean Workers' Party (the official name of North Korea's Communist Party) and to the Great Leader Kim-Il Sung. Those who showed loyalty and devotion during the classes and worked hard in the mines received awards from the Interior Ministry. In order to encourage the other prisoners, a few of the most loyal workers were allowed to live outside the compound with regular North Korean laborers. The extra freedom was a big reward.

On the other hand, those who would not listen and went against the authorities were threatened, and some were given exhausting interrogations until they gave in and submitted.[14] The few who kept resisting, one day vanished. They were probably taken to some bleak prison camps that were even worse than the Kumduck Mine, or they were simply executed.

---

[14] These interrogation sessions were a form of psychological torture designed to drain the victim both physically and mentally. The subject of the interrogation is forced to sit in an office for several hours straight while various officials and Party members come in and take turns yelling at the victim and making threats.

All the POWs had to work their tails off just to survive. We had to fulfill our quotas no matter what. But I was willing to do whatever it took to survive and return home to the South to my family.

A few seemed to have just given up on making it out. Others naively believed everything that the North Koreans told them, and worked really hard. But who could blame them—they, too, were only trying to survive.

We were always being watched, so we had to be careful about everything we said. We were forbidden to talk about our prisoner status, our hometown, and especially about repatriation—these were all sensitive matters. If someone did talk about any of these things, he would be subject to a session of self-criticism for ideological weakness.

Self-criticism sessions involved being put in front of a crowd of people who would make you reprimand and insult yourself for hours, sometimes until you got sick. This would be difficult under any circumstances, but after long hours of hard labor, such sessions would make your legs stiff and make you feel nauseous. You would get yelled at and chewed out so much, you felt like you were going to be killed right there.

Making excuses for your faults was not allowed. If you were stupid enough to give an excuse, you would be lambasted even more for being unrepentant. Thus you had to admit being guilty to all of the accusations and sometimes make up crimes that you never committed. It was psychological torture—just as bad, if not worse, than working in the mines.[15]

Even a slip of the tongue in a casual conversation could lead to a self-criticism session. Some of the prisoners who wanted to curry favor with the government reported other prisoners' mistakes to internal security. Soon, if you were in a conversation with someone else and you spoke about a sensitive matter, you had to tell on the other person before he told on you. We could no longer trust one another. This was just what the North Koreans wanted.

I realized that in order to survive I could not stand out. I had to be humble and quiet. I was very careful, but even then, I got into trouble once. I often talked to other POWs who were having trouble adjusting

---

[15] Self-criticism was used in many communist countries to make soldiers conform through peer pressure. In North Korea, this practice was also used on civilians in order to make them ideologically uniform. The technique remains in use today. A similar technique called a "struggle session" was used in Communist China during Mao's revolution (1949) and later, and during the Cultural Revolution (1966-76). Struggle sessions included public humiliation in front of screaming mobs of up to 100,000 people and frequently climaxed in executions. Many victims of struggle sessions committed suicide.

to the difficulties of the mine and gave them encouragement. Gradually I gathered a small following. People came to me when they needed advice or encouragement, but some saw this as fomenting unrest and going against the system.

One evening a meeting was called for the laborers. About twenty workers, a staff officer, and the Commissar were in attendance.[16]

"Today's meeting is about organizational problems. Someone among us has been lying about his past and agitating the workers," said the meeting chair. I still had no idea who was supposed to be accused that night. Whenever one of these meetings came up, I would wonder if there was something I had done wrong and mentally rehearse my response should I be the target of one of these seemingly random attacks. But this time I could not think of anything I had done to get me in trouble.

"Young-Bok Yoo is the agitator."

I could not believe my ears. It was happening to *me*! I was the accused. I felt dizzy for a second. I didn't know what I had done wrong, but now I realized that I was the reason for the meeting.

"We already know what you are doing wrong, so confess the truth right now."

I knew this was a setup. If I wanted to get out of this without more trouble, I had to confess and repent without talking back. I did my best to remain calm and wait for the next round.

Several workers began to barrage me with accusations. "Tell us the name of the anti-communist group you joined in Seoul! Confess to us about your activities! Don't try to lie!" They gave me no time to catch my breath. In the middle of this, I realized their accusations weren't specific. This must have meant that they didn't have any real evidence against me. They were just blustering.

Finally it was my turn to speak. During a self-criticism you normally just take the blame and apologize for everything. The more you protested, the worse it would get. But this was different. These accusations were serious enough that even the slightest admission of guilt could get me in deep trouble for being an anti-communist spy.

---

[16] *Commissar*: A political officer assigned by the Party to a government organization to ensure political loyalty. Because of their Party connections, they can at times be extremely helpful in getting work done.

I tried to keep my composure as I stood up. I knew that an apology was expected, but I also knew there could be harsh consequences if I did not firmly defend myself.

"All I have done was to give encouragement to any workers who were having difficulties at work. I did this because I think it is necessary to achieve our quotas. Even one person lagging behind can hurt our collective effort. That's why I try to help those who are having difficulties. The only reason why people gather around me is because I counsel some of the depressed workers. Ask *them* if that is agitation. If we don't help them, it will hurt our organization. As a worker, it is my duty to support the organization. If I am to do that, I have to help out my fellow workers who are having trouble. How is that a crime?"

Luckily, there was no one there to say that I had agitated them. Since nobody could contradict me, I looked my accusers in the eye and proceeded to argue my case.

"Some people are questioning my past, but I'd very much like to know what kind of evidence they have against me. If I really have done something wrong, I will accept any punishment. But falsely accusing another worker truly causes strife within the collective and harms production. So, let's hear it. Which anti-communist organization was I a member of, and what did I do there?"

I tried to act confident, but inside I was terrified. No matter how well I argued, if even one person spoke up, it was obvious that they would be all over me again. That is how these meetings worked. I held my breath and awaited their response. Luckily, there were none. They thought that by pressuring me with empty accusations, they could get some sort of confession out of me. The whole thing probably came about because some people were jealous of me.

When the room became quiet, the staff officer ended the meeting. A few days later, the same officer came to me and offered to transfer me to the nearby Ryong-Yang Mine. I wanted to stay with the friends I had made here, so I turned him down. I did not want to create more difficulties. I intended to use this as a learning opportunity and be more careful in the future so that I could make it out of this hell.

Before I knew it, three years had passed. One day in 1956, all the prisoners in the unit were called to assembly. We were told that there would be a very important announcement. Many had already given up hope of being repatriated. However, any change was welcome—our lives could not possibly get any worse. Colonel In-Ho Jo addressed us:

"In this postwar time, it is important that our republic works hard on reconstruction and improving productivity. We need more young men in every part of society. The cabinet has made a very important decision. I will announce that decision now."

The decision was Cabinet Order 143. It demobilized 80,000 soldiers and reassigned them to production and construction jobs. Also, the Interior Ministry Construction Brigades like ours would be demobilized and we would be released into society. Therefore, the prisoners would be given regular North Korean citizenship papers. We were told to be thankful for being honored with full citizenship.

This was terrible news. This meant we would be stuck in North Korea for good. The last sliver of hope for repatriation had been crushed. Colonel Jo acted like this was a huge honor, but to the prisoners, it meant all hope was lost. For those still awaiting repatriation, it was a terrible blow. But what could we do about it? Our only choice was to accept our fate. Some of the prisoners refused, and they were either executed or sent to a political prisoner camp, which was infinitely worse than Kumduck and a virtual death sentence.

Over the next few days, the authorities began trying to convince us that this was a good thing. They pretended to listen to our grievances, but it was just for propaganda. They told us that since we were now proper citizens, we should work harder and lead upstanding lives. If we worked hard, we might even be made Party members. We could get married and start a family. Once Korea was reunited, we could go to the South and be government officials, they promised.

Ultimately, we knew what they were trying to do. It was tough to keep us under armed guard, and if we were so close to each other all the time, we might riot. Releasing us solved these problems. Now every prisoner had to earn their own livelihood.

Disbanding the "construction brigades" and dispersing the prisoners also hid the fact that there were South Korean POWs being held in North Korea. All evidence of the prisoner-of-war camps would be destroyed.

We prisoners were gradually integrated into North Korean society. To settle us down, the authorities tried to arrange mass marriages for us. However, because we were former enemy soldiers, nobody wanted to marry us. It was already clear to the North Koreans that we would not be accepted by North Korean society.

When the Kumduck local administrators found this out, they worked to hide our prisoner status by calling us "liberated fighters" who had once fought for the South, but then willingly joined the North Korean Army. They went on to stage a pair of well-publicized marriages between two "liberated fighters" (Mr. Jae-Sool Park and Mr. Jung-Ryong Shin) and two respected nurses (Miss Bong-Soon Kang and Miss Ok-Hee Bae), in order to show that we were legitimate. Miss Kang and Miss Bae did not know the true identities of their husbands. The administrators hoped this stage play would calm suspicions about our status, at least within the small town of Kumduck.

10

Survival

If we wanted to survive, we had no choice but to follow orders. Those who rebelled or talked back would one day just disappear. We could not ask what happened to those who vanished. Keeping a poker-face and clamping down on our emotions was a necessity, but deep down we were all angry.

After we got citizenship, we took off our military uniforms and put on civilian clothes. I felt like I was crossing a point of no return, but I hoped that we would at least be under less surveillance and control.

Sadly there was no real change in our daily lives; we went right on toiling in the Kumduck Mine. We simply went from being controlled by the army to being controlled by the mining authorities. There were a lot more indoctrination classes, regulations, and political controls. We were also under constant surveillance by the police. Every false move or slip of the tongue was reported. We were instructed to report on each other.

The constant backbreaking work was getting to me. I knew that if I kept laboring in the mines much longer, I would drop dead from exhaustion. Since I was stuck in North Korea anyway, I thought that it would help me survive if I became a skilled worker. Luckily, becoming a skilled worker was encouraged at the time, and there was a technical school available at the mine. To get in you had to have a middle-school education and pass an entrance exam. Thankfully, I had gone to middle school, so I applied, passed the test, and got in. I began taking night classes and was reassigned to work as an apprentice in the Surveying Department.

There were many technical departments in the mine. Of those, the Surveying Department was not easy to get into. Out of all the former POWs, only three made the cut. During the day, we worked in the mines as surveyor's apprentices, and at night we studied surveying theory in class. This was not easy. Most students did not make it through the entire course. They would miss classes because they were too tired, then they would fall behind, and eventually drop out. But I knew that this was the only way I could survive, so I put my nose to the grindstone and worked hard.

Surveying was both technically and physically difficult. We had to walk back and forth through the mineshafts while carrying heavy surveying equipment. We also had to climb to the tops of mountains to do triangulation surveying.

Kumduck Mine was always expanding, so survey work was in high demand and tricky problems came up often. There were many highly capable surveyors in our department. Some people envied me for my job. In a way, it was a privilege to work as an apprentice surveyor. It was a great opportunity.

At least that's what I told myself during the difficult apprenticeship. After working all day, trainees had to go to class for three to four hours. When we finally got back to the dorms, all there was to eat was a small amount of corn and watered-down soup.[17] I was often tempted to cut classes and grab a few precious hours of rest. But then I would think of the other prisoners who were doing backbreaking labor in mines filled with poisonous fumes. Compared to them, I had it easy. I could take this hardship.

Surveyors played a key role in the mine. When you dig a tunnel, you cannot see where you are going, so all excavation plans depended on the surveyors. The quality of surveying determined the mine's productivity and safety. Surveyors made sure the tunnels were the right size and estimated the amount of ore that was produced. They were also responsible for making highly accurate passageways for the mine tracks. Tunneling just one meter is expensive, so if tunnels did not meet when they were supposed to—after, say, a hundred meters of digging—it amounted to a huge waste.

---

[17] According to *Stories about North Korea*, by Sung-ha Joo (http://blog.donga.com/nambukstory/), the corn available in North Korea would be feed quality elsewhere in the world. The hard kernels must be steamed like rice. Well-to-do North Koreans mix some rice with the corn, while poorer families add potatoes or any other scraps. It is the staple food in much of North Korea.

Of the entire technical staff, surveyors were probably the most important to management. I realized that if I became a good surveyor, I could survive in North Korea, and maybe even live pretty well, so I made surveying studies my top priority. One by one, the other students dropped out, but I knew just how important my success as a surveyor was. I *had* to learn this skill. It was a literally a matter of life and death.

If I hadn't been so tired all the time, the studying itself would have been interesting and not too difficult. I had always wanted to further my education, but in the South I could only attend night school, because I had to take part in supporting my family along with my father. However, thanks to the night school, I was now able to study to become a surveyor. It was ironic that it was in the hellish North that I finally got the opportunity to learn.

I was able to obtain my surveyor's license five and a half years later, but only three and a half of those years were actually spent in school. Tuberculosis claimed a few months of my life. I was also very busy finding a wife and starting a family.

During those five years, accidents and exhaustion claimed the lives of many of my friends in the mines. I felt blessed to escape the hard labor. When I got my license, my friends all congratulated me, but I could tell they were a little envious, too. I tried to inspire hope by telling them privately that we were definitely going to be repatriated someday. "The day is going to come when the Republic of Korea brings us home," I said, "so we just have to survive a little bit longer."

But I could tell that a lot of my friends had already given up. Without a second thought, North Korea had violated international law by refusing us repatriation. They had conscripted us into the construction brigades and then made us citizens without giving us a choice. But nobody could speak up about this atrocity—if you resisted you would either disappear or be publicly executed as an example.

11

Tearful Reunion

Back in 1952, when I returned from Koje-Do, I learned that my dad had already sent my mother and four younger siblings[18] to my mother's home village in Yeon-An County, near Haeju, to avoid the fighting. When they went there, the area was under South Korean control. But in 1957, I learned that communist forces had recaptured Haeju and its vicinity by the time of the armistice.[19] I realized that if my mother was still living in Yeon-An at the time of the ceasefire, I might get to see her for the first time in seven years. But at the moment, I had no idea if she was even alive.

I went to the mine headquarters and asked if they could help me find my mother. I gave them her personal details, and one week later they told me yes, she was alive! I thought I was dreaming. My mother, as well as two of my brothers and two of my sisters, were all living in Yeon-An.

While I was overjoyed that I could see most of my family again, this meant that my mother and father had been separated by the Demilitarized Zone (DMZ). I thought of how heartbroken they must have felt when they found themselves split up by the war.

---

[18] At this point, four of the author's five younger siblings are in the North, including his two brothers, Young-Nam and Young-Chul, and two sisters, Gyung-Sook and Myung-Sook. His father and his third sister, Gyung-Eh (the eldest of his siblings, to whom he wrote the ten-page letter when he left to join the South Korean Army) are in the South.

[19] Haeju is north of Seoul, but most families believed that postwar Korea would be a unified Korea, and the rural areas were considered safer, so women and children were frequently sent to rural areas where relatives could help them, even if the location was farther north of Seoul. No one could have imagined that this decision might result in decades of separation after the war.

I had to reconsider my future. Up until then, I had constantly sought a way out of North Korea, hoping to survive until I was repatriated. All I had wanted to do was return to the South. Now that part of my family was in the North, I had to be responsible and take care of them until all of us could be reunited.

I desperately wanted to see them. However, I couldn't just leave Kumduck to see my family whenever I wanted to; I needed permission to travel. So I put in a request to go on leave, and in August—sooner than expected—my request was granted. I sent my mother a telegram and immediately began traveling south, purposely wearing the KPA uniform I had gotten as a construction brigade prisoner, along with a service medal I had earned for my hard work. I wanted to look good in front of my mom and hide my POW status.

At that time in North Korea, anyone wearing a uniform was considered a national hero, but not many soldiers had service medals. The medal was very helpful on the long trip because people treated me respectfully every-where I went.

It took three days of travel by train to reach a station near my mother's village. As I walked down the road lined with pine trees—the same one I had traveled before the war whenever I had visited my relatives in Yeon-An—I found the familiar landscape somewhat depressing, since it reminded me of the time when our family was still together.

The landscape along the sides of the road was in ruins. I heard the old village had been destroyed by bombing, and my mother and siblings were living in a new village nearby. I saw that little village in the distance. Some kids noticed me and started running toward me. I immediately recognized my two pre-teen brothers Young-Nam and Young-Chul.

"Brother!" They called out.

We embraced. My voice was shaking.

Both of my brothers were small, thin, and malnourished. Their clothes were tattered, and it pained me to see them so poor. They took my hand and led me to the village, where I was greeted by what I took to be the entire population. I saw two of my aunts, but where was my mother?

"Your mom is out working in the fields with your sister. She heard you were coming and she will be here soon," said my aunt.

Since it was harvest season, all the adults were working in the fields, leaving only the children and the old in the village. Most of the men had fled to avoid conscription or had died in the war.

The villagers all had something to say:

"We thought you had died."

"This is a such a blessing."

"Your mom has suffered so much—thank goodness there is hope for her."

"Now maybe life will be easier for your mother."

Then one person asked, "We heard that you were separated in the South. How did you end up as a KPA soldier?"

I could not answer him truthfully. I couldn't bring myself to admit that rather than becoming a North Korean soldier voluntarily, I had been dragged here as a POW. I just avoided the question.[20]

"Look! Here comes your mom!"

I turned around and there she was, running toward me with my sister, Gyung-Sook, who was now around twenty years old. Eyes watering, I ran out to meet them.

"You rascal," said my mom. "I thought you were dead, I thought I would never see you again. Do you know how much we've been worrying about you? We were trying to get over you."

Through the tears, I managed to choke out a response. "Mother, you don't have to worry anymore. I'm here now, everything's going to be all right."

I had no idea how I would help my family, but I comforted my mom anyway. She was only fifty-two years old, but the war had been so terrible for her—she was nothing but a pile of bones and her face was filled with wrinkles, as if she were a grandmother.

I was so happy to see my family, but my heart was in turmoil. Up until then, I had cared only about getting back to the South. But if I hadn't been taken prisoner, I wouldn't have been able to see my mother and my younger siblings.

---

[20] There was already a stigma in North Korean society against South Korean prisoners of war.

We were now one of the many families separated by the war.[21] Privately, I wondered if I had to choose right now whether to remain in the North or return to the South, which side would I pick? Whatever side I went to, I knew that I would forever be haunted by the loved ones that I left behind on the other side. Fate was so cruel to me!

After the excitement of seeing each other died down, Mom asked me what had happened to my dad and my sister Gyung-Eh. Though I did not have any recent news, I told her about the last time I had seen them, and that I was sure that they were doing fine in Seoul.

Later on, my younger siblings took me to see where they were living. I was taken toward a small thatched-roof hut. I thought this was my mother's home, but instead they led me past it toward a dugout shelter. *"This can't possibly be where they are living,"* I thought. *"How could any human being stand this?"* But then to my dismay, my brother Young-Nam lifted a rag curtain draped over the mouth of the hollow and stepped inside.

I had to stoop down to get in. It was dark and gloomy. On the ground, a few straw rice bags served as mats. In the corner was a cooking pot, but there wasn't even a proper kitchen. It was barely a hole in the ground.

It had been five years since the end of the war. I had a good grasp of the social structure and realities in North Korea. Over and over in the political indoctrination sessions, they claimed that workers and farmers were the most important elements of society. Didn't they say that the basic needs of the people were being taken care of?

I didn't expect too much, but I couldn't believe my own mother had suffered so much over the past five years. She had been raising my brothers and sisters in this hole in the ground.

My mom told me her story. During the war, she had brought the four youngest children here to her home village, a rural area where she expected it would be safe from the war. She had left my sister Gyung-Eh in Seoul to stay with my father. She was the eldest of the children still with them, virtually as grown up as I was, and could help my father get settled. My mother had believed that she would only need to be in Yeon-An temporarily.

---

[21] It is estimated that almost one million families were separated by the Korean War.

She had heard that a ceasefire had ended the fighting, but did not realize at first that she was now separated from my father and Gyung-Eh, who were still in Seoul. She told me how she waited for my father to come for them after the ceasefire. She would often walk down the pine-tree lined path to the train station, hoping that he would appear. When she learned that the ceasefire had established a DMZ that separated North and South Korea, she had even tried to find a way back to Seoul. She was devastated to learn that it was impossible to cross the DMZ.

She and my siblings became impoverished refugees. Their temporary stay had dragged on for seven years. My mom had not been prepared for such a long stay. By finding work at a nearby farm, she was able to find just enough food to survive.

But even during these difficult times, life went on. My sister, Gyung-Sook, had found a nice fiancé who lived in a nearby village, and the two had married only a few months before I arrived. Gyung-Sook apologized that she had gotten married before me, her elder brother. It was Korean custom for the eldest sibling to get married first. I told her that since they had had no idea if I was alive, she had done the right thing, custom or not, and I gave her my blessing.

I avoided talking about their living circumstances. It hurt to even bring it up, and I knew that it would only make my mom sad. After the war, the local government had rebuilt thatched-roof huts for some of the farmers, but left the refugees to fend for themselves. Since I was a POW, I doubted that anyone would listen to my complaints, but I had to try something.

The next morning I dressed up in my army uniform, went to the farm authorities, and identified myself as the son of Duk-Soon Kang.[22] They saw my uniform and service medal, and, taking me for a regular soldier, were embarrassed. They said that they had had no idea that my mother was the mother of a soldier and apologized for not taking better care of a military family.

I purposely didn't bring up the dugout. Instead, I "thanked" them for taking such good care of my mother and siblings. I told them that after being discharged I was going to be working at the Kumduck Mine and I couldn't come home, so I asked them to please continue to take good care

---

[22] The author's mother's full name. Elders in Korea are rarely referred to by their real names; in the Korean text, this is the only occurrence of the name Duk-Soon Kang.

of them. The manager squirmed with guilt—he apologized over and over again, and then brought up the dugout himself. He promised to do everything in his power to get her a proper home soon. I left the office confident that my mother would be taken care of.

I felt more responsibility since my dad was not around. I was the eldest son, so I had to be the man of the family and take care of my mother, my two brothers, and my two sisters.

12

Matchmaking

Meeting my mother and my four younger siblings gave me a renewed sense of responsibility. To me, family was more important than anything else. The few weeks' time I had had with my family also gave me a sense of calm. I had found my place. Then, a few days later, on a quiet day, my mom brought up my future.

"You're older and mature now, and you've been discharged from the Army. It's about time you started a family of your own. Do you have a girl in mind?"

I was reminded of the marriage problems that had been plaguing me for a while. There had been quite a few prisoners who, thanks to the government, were able to start families. The authorities wanted to convert us prisoners into North Koreans, so they encouraged us to get married.

In fact, there was a girl that I had once been friendly with. She was a nurse at a nearby hospital. We had been close for a while, but I could never ask her to marry me. I could not tell her that I was a prisoner of war.

So I told my mother, "Nobody in particular right now, Mom."

As if she had been waiting for a chance to speak, my mother immediately told me a story about a girl who had helped her survive during the difficult years immediately after the war.

"It was so hard living in this dank and tiny hole, but one of the greatest difficulties was finding food. Some days we didn't even have enough gruel to eat, let alone a decent bowl of rice. Just imagine how it was for your brothers and sisters. But there was this girl who helped us and shared some food with your siblings every time food got short. She's like family."

My mom told me about how the girl lived alone in a hut nearby. Her parents had died when she was young, and her older sister had married and left to live with her husband,[23] so she lived alone and worked in the fields by herself. Her name was Song-Un Hong.

"She's twenty years old, and she's really nice. Not bad-looking either. Why don't you go meet her?"

I felt like I had to meet her, if anything, to thank her for helping my mom. Anyone who helped my family was my friend. Marriage aside, I wanted to see her.

When I agreed to meet her, my mom was ecstatic. She really wanted to see me get married. As it was nearing the end of my leave from work, we lost no time in setting up a formal meeting. On a hot August day, Song-Un and I met at my aunt's house, along with Song-Un's older sister, and some other village women in attendance.[24] Song-Un's sister started the conversation. She spoke about how she worried about her younger sister trying to survive on her own, and was humble about her sister's shortcomings as a potential wife. She hoped that I could guide her and we could start a successful family.

When it was my turn to speak, I spoke about my own difficulties and shortcomings as a potential husband. I chose my words carefully, since I did not want to seem arrogant. Then came Song-Un's turn to speak. She was very shy the whole time and simply said that she agreed with her sister. What this really meant was that she would accept the marriage as long as her sister approved.

Her words and actions were all very proper and polite. You can't tell everything at first glance, but to me she looked like a goodhearted person, and unlike most rural girls, she was quite pretty. If she consented,

---

[23] When a woman gets married, she leaves her birth family and becomes part of her groom's family. The bride usually severs most ties with her birth family, and only returns to her original family for marriages, funerals and notable occasions. However, this traditional practice is in decline as Korea modernizes.

[24] It was common for family members and friends to come and watch formal meetings between a potential bride and groom. These formal meetings were akin to job interviews, where the bride and groom assessed each other for matchmaking purposes. Dating, as we know it in the West, is a relatively new phenomenon in Korea.

I wouldn't mind getting married to her, but I knew that this was not just my decision alone.

Carefully I asked her, "If we were to get married, do you think you would be able to live far up north at a mine in the Hamgyong provinces?"[25]

This was an important question, since many people from the area did not like traveling very far. Also, life near a mine was both dangerous and demanding. Her sister answered for her, saying, "The thread always follows the needle. As long as she is happy, I'm happy."

I wanted to ask Song-Un some more questions to see how she would respond, but she was so shy and innocent that I could not address her directly. The meeting soon ended, and since her sister approved of us being a couple, the marriage was more or less confirmed. All that was left was an engagement ceremony. The problem was that I had come completely unprepared for any ceremony, and there was not enough time, so I had to go home to Kumduck without an engagement.

Soon after I got back, I got a letter from my mother. She said that the two families had discussed everything and agreed that we were a suitable couple, and the next time I came down to visit they would set up an engagement ceremony.[26]

It was truly remarkable. Not only had I been reunited with my mother, but I had found a wife! I had not seen this coming. For so long I had kept myself going on the dream that I would return to the South and to my family. But now, not only had I found family here, but I was about to start a family of my own. I had had no idea that fate would lead me this way.

---

[25] Being remote, mountainous, and cold, North Hamgyong Province and South Hamgyong Province are not unlike North Dakota and South Dakota in the United States, and are often collectively referred to as "the Hamgyong provinces," just as North Dakota and South Dakota are often called "the Dakotas."

[26] In Hwanghe Province, where Haeju is located, marriages had separate engagement and wedding ceremonies.

13

Settling Down

Back in Kumduck, many of my POW friends told me how fortunate I was to have met my mother and brothers and sisters. They also told me how much they missed their own families.

I began studying harder, with a new sense of purpose and responsibility. I also worked hard as a surveyor's apprentice because I wanted to be recognized as a skilled surveyor in the future. This was the only way I could build a good life for my family—my mother, my younger siblings, and the new family I would start with Song-Un.

One by one, my friends had left the mine dormitories to start their own families. I decided that it was time for me to do the same. I planned another trip to see my mother and officially get engaged to Song-Un. After less than a year, I managed to get another leave in June of 1958, and soon I was hurrying toward Yeon-An.

When I arrived, I was glad to find my mom living in her new thatched-roof hut. Although we weren't formally engaged, Song-Un had already accepted me as her groom. She was welcoming and treated me with affection and kindness. She made me feel as if I was already her husband.

My relatives and relatives-to-be not only wanted an engagement ceremony during this trip, but a wedding, as well. I was a little hesitant at first, as I had only planned on getting engaged on this trip. Also, it was June—planting season for rice—so everyone was already very busy. And to be honest, I had not prepared myself for such a big responsibility just yet.

But it was not just the villagers who wanted a wedding. The Farm Committee actually approached me and told me they could set everything up for me. They really encouraged that we get married now and told me it was the smart thing to do, since I would have to make another trip if I did not. "Why don't we just have your engagement and your wedding at the same time!" they suggested.

I thought about it and found myself agreeing with them. There seemed to be no point in delaying when we already had everyone's blessing.

The ceremony was fairly plain, with only a few guests from the village and the Farm Committee. I was a little disappointed by the simplicity of the wedding. I was not even able to afford a photographer, and I still regret not having our picture taken that day. For the next few days, we stayed at my mother's house because I did not have a house of my own in Yeon-An, and we could not afford a honeymoon.

When my vacation was over, Song-Un had to stay behind because there was nowhere for her to stay at Kumduck. I was still living in a miners' dorm. I asked her to stay with my mother while I found a house for us, and told her I would try to come back for her next spring. Many prisoners were getting married, so housing was in short supply in Kumduck, but the government planned to build many new houses by spring.

I headed back to Kumduck without Song-Un. When I got there, I felt elated: I was going to have a family! At the same time, I felt weighed down by my new responsibilities. The sorry reality was that I had very little money and limited prospects. My salary was meager, and once I paid room and board just for myself, there was hardly anything left. I worried about how I could afford a house for both of us and how we could make a living when I was merely a poor surveyor's apprentice.

Then, on December 17, I got a short telegram: "*12/15 Song-Un on way*"

My wife had left Yeon-An to join me in Kumduck on December 15. It caught me by surprise. "*Why couldn't she wait?*" I wondered. "*Winters here are so cold, and I don't even have a room for her; I'm still in the dorms. I told her I would come fetch her in the spring once I had every-thing ready.*" I did not know what to do.

I went to the dormitory cook-mother,[27] who was a trusted friend, and asked her for advice. She warmly told me not to worry and gave me encouragement. She said that my wife and I were both able-bodied people and we would find a way. She told me to be happy that my wife was coming to be with me and to be sure to make Song-Un feel welcome. She then told me Song-Un could stay with her family until I got a house. When she said this, I was deeply grateful, so grateful I almost cried.

The cook-mother had lost her husband in the war and was trying to support her two young children. She was exceptionally kind to us miners. Many times she had helped me before, and I respected her a great deal. Now I found myself indebted to her again.

The next morning, the train came to Kumduck Station. Kumduck was the end of the line, so everyone had to get off. Amid the crowd of people I saw Song-Un, carrying a small bag. The surroundings were cold and desolate. I could not imagine how she felt and how difficult the journey had been, traveling on a train for three days all by herself, just to see me. I greeted her and took her to the cook-mother's home. The cook-mother was overjoyed to see her and treated her like her own daughter, with lots of love and enthusiasm. Thanks to her, my wife seemed a bit relieved.

I asked Song-Un why she had come here so suddenly. She explained, "The villagers suggested that I go to Kumduck before spring, even if it is tough here. That way I can help out during the spring planting season, and also help get us settled here before it gets busy."

In a way, I was glad that she was determined to come to Kumduck and help out. I understood why she had come, but that did not make our situation any easier—I did not even have a house for her to stay in. The cook-mother seemed to understand my anxiety, and reassured both of us that she would let my wife stay with her until I found a home. I sent a telegram to my mother saying that Song-Un had arrived safely.

Trying to start a family without the means to do so was extremely taxing. My body was getting weaker every day. My mind was always stressed over how I was going to support my mother and my siblings as well. I did not feel ready for such responsibilities. I thought fondly of my childhood, when I had no responsibilities. When I was kid, I had always

---

[27] According to Korean custom, elders are never referred to by their names. They are called "aunt" or "uncle," or if they are quite close, "mother" or "father." The author refers to the cook as "mother" because of their close relationship.

wanted to be an adult, but being an adult was hard. An adult needed to make decisions for himself and had to be responsible for his family.

I was reminded of my father. What would he have done in my position? I remembered how hard he worked to support the family. Then my thoughts would wander. Did he think that I had been killed? It seemed more than likely that he must. How could he imagine that I had managed to find Mother, and even get married in the North? What about my sister Gyung-Eh? Was she all right? I was always worrying about both sides of the family, North and South.

This was the bruising pain known only to separated families.

14

TB

Now that my wife was with me in Kumduck, I needed to find a new house as soon as possible. I went to the authorities almost every day, but they told me I had to wait until spring. Since it was wintertime, there weren't any homes for sale. Nobody was looking to move.

January of 1959 at Kumduck was particularly chilly.[28] My wife said she had never experienced such cold weather before. Then, that month, the cook-mother told us that someone she knew was being relocated, and I managed to obtain the housing permit for their soon-to-be-vacant house.[29] As soon as her friend left, I would have a home.

In February, the cook-mother's friend left and we were able to move in. All we could afford in the way of furnishings were a few rice bowls. My mother sent us the bedding that we had received as a wedding gift. Also, the previous owner had left a large pot and a big rice jar behind. These helped us get started. At the time, the North Korean food distribution system worked well, and we could also get coal from the government. Even though we did not have much, we hoped that life would improve, and we wanted to make our families proud.

But just as we were trying to get settled, I began to feel profoundly fatigued. I thought it was just because I was under a lot of stress, but it got

---

[28] As noted earlier, winters in Kumduck can reach -35°F.

[29] A government permit was required in order to live in a house.

worse, and soon I couldn't get out of bed. I discovered that I had contracted tuberculosis. I wanted to hide this from my wife since I didn't want her to worry after she had traveled so far for me. But the local hospital could not treat me. If I wanted to recover, I had to go to a special, faraway clinic for a three-month-long treatment. I didn't know what to do.

Again, I sought the cook-mother's advice. She told me to stop worrying about my TB and *do* something about it. She reminded me that the only way for me and my wife to have a good future was for me to be healthy. However, I found it difficult to break the news to her because I was worried that she would feel let down and disappointed. The next day, the cook-mother called Song-Un to her house to break the news to her. "Your husband has gotten sick because he has been working and studying so hard," she said. "He needs to go to a special hospital for three months to get better. During that time, I'll take care of you. I know this is going to be hard for you, but for you folks to be happy, he needs to be healthy. After all, in the long run, three months is a short time. I'm sure you can handle it."

A lot of people were suffering from TB, so the hospitals were overflowing with requests for treatment. The provincial hospital where I was admitted held about 200 male and 100 female patients, most of whom were middle managers and junior Party members. Only a few people from Kumduck Mine were admitted per month. Since I was a skilled worker and a former "soldier" in the construction brigades, I was one of the fortunate few.

The hospital was comfortable. The patients were given good food— real rice and side dishes—and good treatment.[30]

North Koreans remember the 1960s as a golden age, when North Korean life was at its best. The hospitals were well-run and free. I could focus on getting healthy. I listened closely to treatment instructions and also learned how I could stay healthy after leaving the hospital. TB is difficult to fully cure, so you have to stay healthy and keep it suppressed, even after the three-month treatment.

Gradually, my condition improved, until I was able to take walks in the surrounding hills and do some light exercise during leisure time.

---

[30] Rice without corn mixed in was a luxury.

My wife came to visit in April. While I was surprised and glad that she had come, I was also worried because I had wanted to keep her from knowing that I was sick with TB—I did not want her to worry about me. We spent some time together in the garden. Song-Un was smiling, and she said that I looked much healthier, but I could tell that she was holding back tears. Behind her smile, she was really worried.

"I'm gonna be okay soon. You didn't have to come here," I said.

Song-Un told me that the cook-mother had helped her find a temporary job as a laborer, hauling gravel and sand for construction material. When I commented that it must be hard work, she told me that compared to the farm work she had done back home, it was okay, and it gave her something to do. The cook-mother had told her that in these mining towns, it was better if both the husband and wife worked. My wife then gave me some snacks that she had bought with her wages. I was extremely touched.

That evening, my wife wanted to stay a bit longer. There was a lodge for visitors, but I sent her home on the night train since it would not help either of us if she stayed. I was sad to see her go. After she left, I followed the treatment instructions even more carefully, and did everything I could to make sure I got better. She had given me something to live for.

15

A Death in the Family

After three months, I was released from the hospital. During my recovery I had had a lot of time to think about my future. In the end I became firm in my decision to put down my roots here in Kumduck and start a family.

Two months or so after I got back, we went to the photographer and got our picture taken. It was the first photo we had ever taken together. We sent a copy to our families in Yeon-An, along with some clothes as a gift. We were really proud. This was the first time we'd sent something back home. I later learned that my mother was very pleased to receive our presents. I hoped that the time would come when we could all live together.

But it was not meant to be. In early November, I received a telegram telling me that my mother was extremely sick. I tried to rush down to Yeon-An as quickly as I could, but the trains were delayed. When I got there, I could tell from the expressions of the people in town that I had arrived too late. My mother had passed away on November 5, 1959.

I remembered how happy my mom had been when I first showed up. She had always worried what would happen to my siblings if she were to die. Now that I was here, she had joked, she could die in peace whenever she wanted to. I still heard her voice in my head.

We buried her next to her parents at the family burial ground.[31] As we laid her to rest, I thought to myself, *"Rest in peace, mother. I will take care of my brothers and sisters. I'm sorry I couldn't make you happier while you were alive."*

It was too much to lose her again. I felt so bad that she was never able to be reunited with Dad. She was only fifty-three years old when she passed away. At least she was wearing the dress we had sent her when we laid her to rest.

At twenty-nine years old, I was now the head of my entire family. After the simple funeral, I notified the authorities that my mother had died and prepared the paperwork so that three of my siblings could come with me to Kumduck. My twenty-two-year-old sister Gyung-Sook, who was already married and settled in Yeon-An, wasn't coming with us. After a tearful goodbye with all of our friends and relatives, we left the village.

With my two brothers Young-Nam and Young-Chul, and my eight-year-old sister Myung-Sook, in tow, I returned to Kumduck. My wife was surprised to see them, and when she learned that my mother had died, she was devastated that she had been unable to go down and attend her funeral. Later that evening I sat down with my wife and three younger siblings—my new family—and spoke to them in a fatherly manner, trying to encourage them.

"There is no time left to feel sorry for ourselves. The way we can fulfill mother's wishes is to look out for each other and stick together as a family. This is a tough time, but we have each other. Let's support each other and get through this."

We decided to proceed with hope. Luckily, my wife was already close to my siblings. They treated her like another mother. However, there were a lot of difficulties in caring for a bigger family. Our house was too small, and although we received a little extra food for child support, it was not nearly enough to feed three growing kids. I felt so helpless and heart-broken because I could see that they were always hungry. I really wanted to do something for them, but with my measly pay there was very little I could do. I did manage to buy a goat that provided us with milk. It helped a little bit, but I always wanted to do more for them.

---

[31] In Korea, rural families each had private burial areas.

The five of us became a tight and close-knit group, all working together to make a livelihood. Young-Nam and Young-Chul were in high school and Myung-Sook was in middle school. I hoped they could get an education so they weren't condemned to mine labor for the rest of their lives. When they got home from school, they helped around the house, doing chores and feeding the goat. My wife got a job cutting hair at a children's barbershop, which was much better than her previous job as a regular laborer. We coordinated our days off so that we could all go cut firewood or prepare goat feed together. I was proud to be part of a hard-working, well-adjusted family.

The whole time, my status as a POW was hidden from my family. Nobody knew the true details of my past, and they never asked. I knew that eventually my three younger siblings would grow up and find out for themselves. I decided that before that happened I would work hard and make a name for myself in North Korea as a citizen.

At the political indoctrination classes, we were taught that if you worked hard, you could be admitted to the Party, regardless of your past. With this in mind, I kept my hopes up. But deep down, I knew that admission to the Party was nothing more than a distant dream. Realistically, there was almost no chance.

16

Trying to Become a Party Member

Many other POWs had also started families of their own, and many had kids. Most of my fellow POWs were mine laborers. But we all tried to stay hopeful for the sake of our families. We realized that it would be hard to get back home, so we decided to work hard and try to gain admittance to the Party.

The most important thing in North Korea was your political classification, which was determined by your family's political status, your own political status, and whether or not you were a Party member. If you were a Party member, you would be treated well wherever you went. But if you were not, it was really hard to get ahead in society. It did not matter how smart or talented you were—if you were not a Party member, you would not be recognized. Over time, the difference between castes would only grow more and more conspicuous.

Perhaps more important for POWs was that Party membership could help our children avoid discrimination. It was hard enough to be a child of a non-Party member, but it was even worse if you were the child of an enemy soldier. By becoming a Party member, we thought perhaps our children could avoid the stigma of our own POW status.

The government propaganda claimed that anyone who worked hard and stayed loyal to the Party could become a member. Many young people with a "complicated"[32] political classification, including POWs, were obsessed about being admitted to the Party. They always volunteered for the most dangerous jobs because there was a special admission process[33] for people who did miraculous things. Such people could be admitted to the Party regardless of their political classification. Unfortunately, this was highly uncommon. For many, it was a dream that became a nightmare: countless POWs were killed while taking on deadly jobs in hopes of a "battlefield promotion." Their dying wish was to be named a Party member after they were dead and buried.

There was also an unofficial age limit on being admitted to the Party. Typically, inductees were in their late twenties or early thirties. They were young enough to be exploited further. Once someone was past their early thirties, it was almost impossible to gain admission. This age limit made attaining Party membership all the more difficult.

Kumduck Mine was immense and had a long history. The mine tunnels stretched deep into the mountain, so just getting to the end of a tunnel could take a while. We worked around the clock in three eight-hour shifts. There was always blasting going on, so the air was always bad. There were fatal accidents nearly every day. It got to the point where any word of an accident meant that someone had died, since broken bones and similar injuries were not even considered accidents. Blasting accidents caused most of the deaths, but many people also died because of cave-ins and suffocation by methane gas.

It got so bad that Kim Il-Sung visited Kumduck Mine on April 5, 1961. He instructed us not to collect ore that had bloodstains on it because blood could permanently dye the ore. Because mineral production from Kumduck was a big part of North Korea economy, he encouraged us to

---

[32] All "complicated" individuals—people the government considered politically unreliable—automatically belonged to a low social status. The ranks of the complicated were made up of South Korean POW families and other suspect groups, such as families of people who had opposed the communists when they took power in 1948, and families with members who had been punished for political crimes. The classification also included less obvious groups, such as the families of pro-communist ethnic Koreans who voluntarily migrated to North Korea from Japan in the 1960s. Though the number of people who are considered complicated is not known, some estimates range as high as 20 to 30 percent of the population. See the U.S. State Department's *2004 Country Report on Human Rights Practices*, http://www.state.gov/j/drl/rls/hrrpt/2004/41646.htm

[33] This admission process, *hwa-sun ip-dang*, literally means "line-of-fire Party promotion." It is like a battlefield commission, in which even a private can be promoted to an officer without formal training. Becoming a Party member by special admission was the happiest event in the lives of many North Koreans.

produce more. It was his "on-the-spot guidance."[34] Later, in 1970, he also told us to work harder and increase the production of zinc from 100,000 tons a year to 300,000 tons a year. Because of the importance of the mine, there were always high-ranking Party officials directing our work.

The "Chollima"[35] campaign, which began in 1960, was an increased production drive undertaken by all of North Korea. That, along with Kim Il-Sung's April 5th mandates for Kumduck, drove increased demand for work. The Party claimed that hard workers during this campaign would be considered for special Party membership.

Encouraged by this, many former POWs worked especially hard. The conditions inside the mineshafts were torturous. Even just standing inside the deep shaft was suffocating and would cause you to become drenched in sweat. After working awhile, we would not be sweating anymore. It was as if our bodies had run out of sweat. The salt on our shirts left from the sweat would leave rashes on our skin.

In spite of the horrible conditions, the POWs volunteered to eat and sleep inside the sweltering mines for days at a time. Kitchens and rest areas were even set up inside mineshafts. Many miners would not see sunlight for days. After a few days of this hell, workers looked wretched and destroyed, but we kept pushing ourselves in these conditions with the hope of becoming an "exemplary worker" and being admitted into the Party. We POWs were by far the hardest working and most loyal workers at the mines.

But very few POWs were ever made Party members. Far more of them died during this time. Many others got sick with lung disease, joint disorders, and other chronic illnesses. Even the POWs who became Party members were only showpieces and were never given any real authority. But the mere fact of having Party membership looked good on the surface. At least their children did not seem to feel as much shame as the children of other POWs.

---

[34] North Korean leaders often visited industrial and production centers to give "on-the-spot guidance." Such "guidance" had the force of an order.

[35] Literal translation: *thousand-li horse*. A thousand li is roughly 400 kilometers, a distance comparable to the distance between Washington DC and New York (320 kilometers). The term refers to a legendary breed of horses that can run 400 kilometers in one day. Historically, only horses used by the royal courier service had such stamina and speed.

69

I came to realize that the Kumduck Mine was itself a gulag.[36] POWs were not the only people who were being punished there. Political prisoners—people who made a mistake somewhere high up—were often sent to Kumduck as punishment. Kumduck's nickname was "the furnace for political correction."

One of those who comes to mind is General Bang Ho-San. He had been a war hero. At the age of fifteen, he had joined Mao Zedong's guerillas and fought against the Japanese imperialists. He then led KPA troops during the Korean War. After the war, he became the dean of the Military Academy. He was so famous that he was in the North Korean textbooks. However, even *he* somehow fell out of favor with Kim Il-Sung. He was sent to Kumduck and worked in the mines for a while, until he disappeared.[37]

This was only one example out of many that the only way to survive in North Korea was to keep your mouth shut and do as you were told. Your entire life could be ruined by one slip of the tongue. Even in Kumduck, which was a hell all by itself, those who spoke up or protested would disappear. They were probably taken to a political prisoner camp, which was even worse than the virtual POW camp that was Kumduck. No one knew for sure what happened to them because those who tried to find out disappeared, too. No matter how high or low you were in the political caste system—whether you were a war hero or an enemy prisoner of war—there was always a deeper level of hell into which you could fall.

---

[36] The *Gulag* was a vast network of forced labor camps set up in the former USSR by dictators Lenin and Stalin, whose horrors are vividly described by Alexander Solzhenitsyn in *The Gulag Archipelago* (1989).

[37] Some historians believe that Bang later returned to China and died there.

17

Accomplished Surveyor

Finally, five and a half years after beginning the three-and-a half-year surveying course, I got my license. This was imperative to my survival, as it was the only way to avoid doing hard labor in the mines. At the time, the government was encouraging the people of North Korea to become skilled laborers. They gave skilled laborers more food, extra bonuses, and, every few years, gifts of household items and clothes.

Like many other POWs, I worked hard in order to gain admission to the Party and secure a better future for my family. After Kim-Il Sung's on-the-spot guidance in 1970, we had to build new mining facilities to increase production, so there was a lot of challenging surveying work to be done.

Mining in sandy or wet areas demanded a high degree of precision. Any errors could result in wasted effort and loss, and the surveyors would be blamed. When there was complex tunnel surveying, I worked extra hard and went without sleep. I also had to help set up two new ore-processing sites. One of these, Processing Site Number 3, was said to be the largest in Asia. This was all part of the effort to produce 300,000 tons of ore per year.

The government also ordered us to work for the military. One job I was assigned was the surveying work for a bunker near Hamhung, a port city on North Korea's east coast. This bunker had to be very deep and nuclear bomb-proof. I spent a lot of time surveying during the excavation.

Once the excavation was over, my role was completed, and I left with no idea what the bunker was for.

They also needed my skills at the nearby Ko-Won coalmine. At the time, the government was having trouble getting people enough heating coal, so the Ko-Won Mine was opened to the public and citizens were told to mine their own coal. At Ko-Won I met two other surveyors, Won-Shi Kim and Bong-Do Yang. Interestingly, they were both POWs, like me.

Over time, I acquired a lot of surveying experience and became much better at my job. I grew more confident about my surveying abilities, and even received some medals for my work. But surveying was a diverse field, so I still had a lot to learn.

18

Adoption

Time passed, and my sister Myung-Sook and brothers Young-Nam and Young-Chul grew up, got married, and settled down, one by one. Once they left home, my wife and I had less to worry about. But the house was too quiet, because we still didn't have any kids of our own, even though we had been married for ten years.

My wife had always been a reserved person, but recently she had been quieter than usual. I worried that she was getting lonely and depressed because we did not have children. We finally decided to consult the OB/GYN. We were a bit shy at first but the doctor was a skilled and famous physician from Pyongyang. After the checkup, I sent my wife home and the doctor told me the results.

I learned that the medical term for my wife's condition was a "retro-flexion" of her uterus. The doctor told me that her uterus had not fully developed. I got the impression that it would be hard for her to become pregnant, though not completely impossible. But when I got home I did not tell my wife the actual results of the checkup. I was afraid that she would just be let down and depressed if I told her the truth. Instead, I comforted her and said that if she got treatment, there was hope, and that even if she could not get pregnant there was nothing to worry about.

She continued to receive treatment, but it did not help. She worried about it more every day. One day, she even told me that it would be a disaster if my family line was cut off because of her. She even said that

I should find another woman to bear my child, adding that she would be willing to leave if she had to.[38] This was how much this problem worried her.

It tore at my heart that she would say that. After marrying me, she had gone through so much without complaining, and she had even raised my sister and my brothers like they were her own children. She was my wife. I would never divorce her.

My bosses knew my situation and tried to help. They arranged for her to get treated at a special infertility clinic in Joo-Eul, North Hamgyong Province, that offered hot spring therapy. To be honest, I did not expect a miraculous cure, but my wife had high hopes. When the treatment failed to help, she was devastated.

My friends suggested that we adopt a baby. Having a child around would certainly get rid of the loneliness. They also said that a childless couple would sometimes get pregnant after adopting a baby.

My wife was hesitant because she was not sure that she could raise a child when she was not nursing.[39] I told her that other families got adoptions and did just fine. Song-Un agreed, and in 1968, when I was thirty-eight years old, we adopted a one-year-old baby girl born on October 13, 1967. We named her Jung-Mi.

We were happy to have a child, but there were difficulties, especially getting milk. We had to ask for milk from the other nursing mothers in the village, but it was hard to get enough. Jung-Mi wasn't ready for regular milk or porridge. She would often get sick and we would have to take her to the hospital. At the hospital, it was even harder to sterilize the bottles and prepare the milk.

Despite the hardships, we treated her with love and care. My sister and my brothers also loved their new niece, and many of my friends' wives lent their active support. Now there was laughter and joy in our house. The happiness brought by Jung-Mi lessened our stress and worries.

My friends then encouraged me to adopt a boy. They told us that it would be "easy" now that we already had experience raising Jung-Mi. But again, my wife was hesitant at first. The economic situation in North

---

[38] In traditional Korean marriage customs, a wife who could not bear children could be divorced. In modern times, this is rare.

[39] There was no infant formula.

Korea was getting worse, and it was getting harder to find the sugar and sweet rice needed to make baby food. But then came a great event that gave us hope: the July 4th North-South Joint Statement of 1972.

19

July 4th, 1972

On July 4th, 1972, North and South Korea released a joint statement announcing a mutual interest in an independent, peaceful reunification. It was very shocking news. Up until then, we had been told that Communist reunification was the only solution. What's more, the envoy from South Korea who came to the North and spoke with Kim-Il Sung was none other than the head of the hated Korean Central Intelligence Agency (KCIA).[40] We were sure that even if total reunification did not happen soon, there would at least be peace between the two nations.

We all truly believed that soon our borders would open and there would be travel between North and South. It was like a dream come true, especially for the POWs. We were all given a renewed sense of hope. One of my friends even prepared the clothes he would wear when he returned to his hometown in the South. As for my wife and I, we were so encouraged that we adopted a new baby boy, whom we named Jung-Ho.

It would have been great to have open borders, but I did not share in the blind optimism of my friends. I had reservations because the statement did not mention anything specific, so reunification was far from guaranteed. Moreover, I was in no hurry to go to the South at the time. I had a family in the North to look after. If I returned to the South, it would be only after

---

[40] North Korean media and propaganda regularly blasts the KCIA as an evil secret police agency that oppresses the South Korean people, a charge delivered without the faintest hint of irony. Consequently, a visit by the head of the KCIA was a sign of hope for more peaceful relations between the two nations.

total reunification, since I couldn't afford being stranded in the South and separated from my new family.

Soon after the July 4th Statement, the State Security officers (North Korea's secret police) began investigating the South Korean POWs. They called us into their office and asked us some questions, such as whether we had anything troubling on our minds. I, too, was called in, and spoke with an agent for a little while. On the one hand, it seemed like the secret police were being nice for a change; but on the other, they were reminding us that they were watching.[41]

---

[41] Being called in by State Security was always a frightening experience because it entailed the chance that one might be tortured, sent to a prison camp, or even executed. It was remarkably "nice" for State Security to call anyone in and politely ask routine questions.

20

Juche

At the time of the joint statement, the North Korean government started to promote Kim Il-Sung's *Juche* ideology of self-reliance and independence.[42] Among other things, Juche taught that we needed to be agriculturally self-sufficient. North Korea imported most of its phosphate minerals used for fertilizer from Vietnam. In order to become self-reliant, we had to develop phosphate mines of our own.

There was a mine forty kilometers to the southeast from Kumduck toward T'anchon[43] called the Dong-Am Mine, where there were around 200 million tons of phosphorite ore. Dong-Am had been mined during the Japanese occupation, but mining was eventually halted because the ore was poor grade and too expensive to get out of the ground. But despite the costs, the Juche philosophy taught that it was more desirable to produce fertilizer internally than to import it from abroad.

A "1st Class State Enterprise"[44] was quickly put together. Managers and skilled workers were recruited from nearby mines, and farmers and

---

[42] *Juche*, which North Korean texts translate as "independent stand," made its debut in a 1955 speech by Kim Il-Sung. Over a fifteen-year period, Juche evolved into a set of guiding principles, such as a strong military and the development of national resources for self-reliance. It also marked a declaration of ideological independence from the Soviet Union.

[43] T'anchon is a port city along North Korea's east coast.

[44] A "1st Class State Enterprise" is a state enterprise that comprises 5,000 workers and produces an "essential national product". These are the largest and highest priority civilian state enterprises (military enterprises have a separate classification). In contrast, a "2nd Class State Enterprise" employs 3,000 workers.

other workers were drafted from all over South Hamgyong Province. Even students from the prestigious Hamhung Chemical Engineering University came to help. Some managers and surveyors from Kumduck were ordered to come down, too.

For the sake of my children, I too wanted to transfer to the Dong-Am Mine. Moving to a place where nobody knew me would hide the fact that my children were adopted. I wanted people to think that they were my birth children. Also, I hoped that I might be promoted to the Party by special admission. I was a little too old, but the technical work for the surveying at this new mine was going to be difficult, so if I completed it successfully, I thought I had a chance. Finally, I wanted to leave Kumduck, which felt like a prison.

I went to the surveyors' headquarters and asked my manager for a transfer, but he refused to let me go, so I went directly to Mr. Te-Eul Yang, who was to be the head engineer at the new Dong-Am Mine. I begged him to take me with him. Yang knew about my surveying skills and that I was a hard worker, so he agreed to bring me.

In early October, 1972, my family—Song-Un, Jung-Mi, and our newly adopted son Jung-Ho—left the Kumduck Mine where I had lived for over twenty years. Young-Nam, Young-Chul, and Myung-Sook were sad to see me go. We had lived together and struggled together for so long. I was also sad to leave my siblings and friends, but I had to go for the sake of my kids.

At Dong-Am, we were given a home from the government. It was a four-family complex for mineworkers and their families, owned by the Dong-Am Mining Committee.

There was a lot of work to be done at Dong-Am. The surveyors spent all day traversing the mountains and taking triangulation measurements to make topographic maps. We worked hard to get the information prepared so we could begin strip mining.

It began to snow as winter set in, but we could not stop working because of the bad weather. We had to make the maps for the mining to begin. There was also a lot of construction surveying to do, since new houses had to be built for the new workers. There was so much work, and it was so difficult, that I wondered many times if coming to Dong-Am had been a bad idea. I was worried that I might make surveying mistakes.

There were other difficulties. The biggest problem was getting food for Jung-Ho. At Kumduck we could get at least a little milk for him, but at Dong-Am it was impossible to find any. To make matters worse, we were short on all other supplies. But I could not complain—I had *asked* to be moved here.

At Kumduck, there were many POWs. However, there were only a few of us at Dong-Am, so the secret police paid closer attention to us than they had at Kumduck. In the midst of this heightened scrutiny, a POW boiler technician, Choong-Ryul Kim, complained that he did not have a house. He disappeared shortly afterwards.

POWs were discriminated against in other ways, too. My friend Yong-Su Jun made a great contribution to a nearby goldmine, greatly increasing production. However, he only got a medal and was not promoted into the Party. Another POW, Dae-Sung Kang, was a mine designer. He was exploited and overworked, but instead of being rewarded, he was demoted and sent to do hard labor in the mine.

There were seven or eight former POW technical workers in Dong-Am. All of us came there with the hope of getting Party membership, but none of us got in. We were just taken advantage of for our hard work.

21

Pressure

As the senior surveyor at Dong-Am Mine, I was responsible for calculating the mine's total yield and reporting it to headquarters. Survey calculations were all based on science and could not be fudged, but since senior managers were evaluated on the output of their mine, I was pressured to make the numbers look better.

For the first few years, Dong-Am ran smoothly and exceeded quotas. The government was very pleased, and many workers were rewarded for their work. We were successful in the beginning because there was plenty of easily accessible, high-grade ore. But once we had mined out all the easy ore, the output quickly declined.

Kim Il-Sung took great personal interest in 1st and 2nd Class State Enterprises. He received production reports directly from the managers. If a manager failed to meet his quota, he would be kicked out.

Eventually so much soil had to be removed to reach the good ore that the mine's production slowed, and in 1980, we failed to meet the January and February ore quotas. Our charismatic General Manager, Hak-Bum Jo, promised to make up for the lost production in March and meet our first-quarter goals. The fertilizer was greatly needed because the spring planting season was on the horizon. But this was not something that Mr. Jo could accomplish with words alone.

During my apprenticeship, I had been taught that surveying was an objective skill. The most important thing was to calculate accurate numbers. The managers reiterated the need for accuracy. However, the reality was that managers and department heads would try to influence the results. Low-level managers and crew chiefs would use bribes of food and liquor to convince their surveyor to give a more favorable estimate. Higher-level managers would bribe, too, but they could also *threaten* the surveyor.

One day in March, the Chief Engineer, Mr. Te-Eul Yang—the same Mr. Yang who had brought me to Dong-Am from Kumduck—called me into his office. He asked me to measure the ore in the stockyard. This sounded like a routine request on the face of it, but he seemed a little on edge that day. When I returned with the yield numbers, Mr. Yang was waiting for me with the Planning Section Chief. Then he saw the numbers.

"Why are these numbers so small?" he yelled. "We need to reach our production goals this month! General Manager Jo has already reported to the Chairman[45] himself that we would reach our quarterly quota. These numbers are too small! They can't be right!"

I was at a loss for words. The laborers had done all the actual mining. All I was supposed to do was measure the amount of ore after it had been mined. Of course my measurements were not *completely* accurate—they might be off by as much as few hundred tons of ore—but I was not off by several *thousand* tons, as Mr. Yang was arguing.

He told me that regardless of our actual production yield, I needed to make "adjustments" so that we could reach our quarterly goals. He said that it would be fine to do so because we could just increase production next month to make up for this month.

I objected. "Sir, I have measured the ore as accurately as possible. There aren't any adjustments to be made."

"I don't think you understand me. We've already reported that we would meet this month's production goals!"

"My signature goes on the reports. I won't lie about the figures."

"Don't you get it? It's fine if we fudge the numbers because next month we will mine more and it will automatically even out!" he yelled.

"And what do we do if we don't make our quota next month, either?"

---

[45] One of North Korean leader Kim Il-Sung's many titles, this one echoing that of Chinese Communist Party Chairman Mao-Zedong.

We argued back and forth for a long time, but I refused to lie about the production yield. Though nobody would come here and measure or weigh the ore in person, at some point it could be revealed that the numbers had been faked. If that happened, who would get the blame?

I told him that I was sure my figures were correct, and if he wanted a second opinion, he should ask a surveyor from a different mine. But Mr. Yang was determined to have me falsify the numbers. He kept pressuring me. I was sure that General Manager Jo had given him strict orders to get the right numbers out of me. Mr. Jo could be likable, but he was also ruthlessly ambitious and very vain. He was willing to throw other people under the bus to get ahead himself.

I refused to change the production yield. It was my principle—not only a principle of integrity, but a principle of survival. My status as a former POW meant that I would never be forgiven for lying about the numbers.

A few days later, Mr. Jo returned from Pyongyang. The first thing he did when he came back was to open a self-criticism session against me. He branded me an incompetent and negligent surveyor. The self-criticism had a script, and I was the scapegoat. After several of his cronies loudly accused me, it was my turn to speak, and I did not try to defend myself.

"I'm not perfect, and I'm no surveying professor. I can't say that every job I do is going to be done right. I think I failed to get the right numbers because of my limited skill. I will accept any punishment for my lack of ability."

The sentence was simple. Since I was too incompetent to be a surveyor, they kicked me out of the Surveying Department and made me a regular laborer. The injustice of the punishment was painful to bear, but there was nothing I could do. I had simply lost a fight against people with far greater power than me. *"I'm getting too old to handle the pressure anyway,"* I told myself. My wife worried a great deal for me. She was sad that I would have to do hard labor in such poor health.

Two months later, a South Hamgyong Province Auditor came to the Dong-Am Mine. Auditors were often sent by the central government to visit the big state enterprises and check their books. They had a lot of authority and could often help important projects get through. However, this auditor was from the Provincial Prosecutor's Office. Auditors from the Prosecutor's Office only came to investigate when something was wrong.

A few days after he arrived, the auditor, Mr. Haw, came to the construction site I was working at and spoke with me.

"You used to be the highly regarded senior surveyor at Dong-Am. Why are you doing labor at a construction site now?" he asked me.

"I'm getting old. I can't do detailed measurements and calculations, so they put me here, where it's less stressful," I said.

Mr. Haw left with a confused expression.

I had a hunch that auditor Haw had been sent to investigate a discrepancy in the Dong-Am Mine ore production figures. But I had to be careful with what I said because I didn't know which side the auditor was on. If I said the wrong things, I could get in a lot of trouble. It was safest to stick to the "official" version of the story.

A few days later, Mr. Haw came to me again.

"What was the ore inventory that you reported to the mine in March?"

"I don't have the figures now, but I have records in my memo book. I can tell you once I find it."

After refusing to falsify the production numbers, I had kept a copy of my calculations in my memo book, just in case something like this was to happen. Actually, Mr. Haw should have been able to obtain my calculations from the Surveying Department.

I told Mr. Haw that I had reported my survey results to the Department, but they had said that the numbers did not make sense. They said there were a lot of errors and sent me here for being negligent.

Somewhat later, I was told to attend a meeting for Party officials and mine executives. The meeting began with an audit report summary. The actual amount of ore in the stockyard was 2,000 tons less than the yield that the mine reported. After the report, an inquiry was held. None of the managers at the mine could properly explain what had happened to 2,000 tons of ore. Some managers sheepishly explained that it must have been blown away by the wind.

"Are you kidding me!" Mr. Haw bellowed angrily. "This is *two thousand tons* we're talking about here! Two thousand tons doesn't just blow away! Can anyone here give me a reasonable explanation? If not, someone must have made a fraudulent report! Whoever did this will be severely punished!"

None of the managers could respond. The auditor then asked them why I had been fired. The surveying section chief stood up and gave some weak explanations. Then Mr. Haw told me to testify.

I had not prepared anything for this meeting, so I was surprised, but I decided to simply tell my story.

I spoke carefully. "My numbers must have been inaccurate. It seems to have caused a lot of confusion here. I'm very sorry. Since this happened in the past, I'd like to move on and continue working hard at my new post."

Mr. Haw did not say anything. Everyone seemed to already know the truth behind what had really happened to me. The Secretary of the Party yelled at the section chief, telling him he needed to be more careful. The section chief just hung his head in silence. I felt a wave of relief. It almost brought a tear to my eye; I had been vindicated.

Finally, it had been revealed that my surveying had been accurate after all. I knew that if I had given in to the pressure from the managers and signed the false numbers, I would have been alone on the chopping block. It was clear that nobody would have defended me and said that I had been pressured into signing the numbers. Even if they had felt sorry for me, nobody could have saved me. I was lucky to have dodged another bullet.

I was told to leave the meeting, but I found out later that several managers had been punished and fined. There was a sharp criticism overall. Also, I was to be reinstated at the Surveying Department.

The Labor section chief called me in to reinstate me a few days later, but I turned down the offer. I had already decided that now that I was fifty, I would rather work as a construction laborer. But then Mr. Jo, the boss himself, the one who reported directly to Kim Il-Sung and had opened the self-criticism session against me, called me in. He acted as if he had done nothing wrong, and he asked me personally to return to the department. He blamed the whole affair on the other managers. He said he needed me; there were going to be a lot of big projects to do soon.

It was an offer from the top that I could not refuse. The next day I was back at the Surveying Department. The other surveyors apologized for what I had gone through. They had done nothing to help me, but they hadn't had the power to do anything, either.

I am still glad that I did not cave in to the managers. I surely would have been punished, and in my bad health, I probably would have died. It was a close call.

22

Recognition

The Dong-Am Mine had a major problem. All the easy ore had already been strip-mined. Now we needed to get to the harder-to-dig ore that was buried underneath a deep layer of dirt. For every ton of ore mined, we needed to excavate one ton of useless dirt.

The Central Mining Research Center in Pyongyang had a new idea. Their plan was to use an enormous amount of explosives to quickly remove all of the dirt covering the ore in one blast.[46] Dong-Am would become the first mine in North Korea to try this new technique. The plan was to remove three million tons of dirt all at once.

It would take six months to prepare for the blast. We needed to dig 1500 meters of complex tunnels in order to accurately place the explosives deep inside the mountain. We were going to use 600 tons of explosives, and we had to make sure none of it went to waste. That was why there was so much work for the surveyors.

I was the lead surveyor for this project. We even had a ceremony where I was given an odd title, "Technical Company Commander." I was put in charge of a special task force assigned to this job (the rest of the miners would continue the difficult strip-mining). I was under a lot of pressure; I had to do the job right. I was honored that the managers had so much faith

---

[46] A similar technique called mountaintop removal (MTR) has recently been used to extract coal in the Appalachian Mountains in the United States.

in me, but I wondered if I could perform my job successfully. Nobody had done mountaintop-removal blasting before.

Anyone involved in mining in North Korea was paying close attention to the outcome of the project. Even the Central Party in Pyongyang had high hopes about this. If this experiment went well, it would be a technical revolution that greatly increased production. Other mines would follow our lead if we got this done right.

On a personal level, I felt this could be my last chance to be considered for Party membership. Pretty soon I would be too old to do anything fantastic enough to be worthy of admission to the Party. I put every ounce of energy I had into the work, eating and sleeping at the worksite, and planning the tunnels for the special taskforce to dig. The taskforce miners worked in three shifts, but I had to be there to direct all three. I could only come home for short periods on weekends. The mine itself became my home.

After six months of non-stop work and 1,500 meters of tunneling to build twenty explosive sites throughout the mountain, we were ready. Researchers from the Central Mining Research Center came to inspect our work. Surveyors and skilled workers from other mines also came as observers. After a thorough inspection, the researchers gave us the all-clear to begin placing explosives.

We began placing the 600 tons of explosives in the explosive sites, which in itself took a long time. The blast tunnels had to be thin and small, so workers had to crawl through to get to the explosive site. Finally, we were all set. The national television station came to film the explosion, and the national newspaper also showed up to report on the removal. With every miner in North Korea watching, the explosives were set off.

The ground shook beneath my feet as explosives at each of the twenty sites in the mountain detonated in sequence like clockwork. The perfectly timed and controlled explosions caused a huge landslide. The top twenty feet of the mountain slid off, exposing the rich phosphate underneath. It looked like the mountain had just taken off its hat.

The mountaintop removal was a complete success. It greatly helped the miners, who could now meet their production quotas. The government dispensed a huge reward. However, this reward was given only to the managers. All I got were a few small medals and a pat on the back. Although I didn't get into the Party, I was glad that I got the recognition and praise from my peers. Most of all, I was relieved that the project had gone smoothly and nobody had been hurt.

23

Retirement

All the POWs worked hard for their captors, the North Koreans. We had been told that if we worked hard, we would be treated fairly. Instead, we were exploited. Few prisoners were ever given proper treatment by the North Koreans. As they passed from youth into old age and lost their usefulness, they became despised and unwanted.

Before I knew it, I had, like most of the other surviving POWs, reached the mandatory retirement age of sixty. By the time I had to retire, many POWs who had become skilled workers had already passed away due to exhaustion.[47] These people died without having fulfilled their greatest wish—to see their beloved homeland again.

A huge accident at Dong-Am in the fall of 1987 shows how easy it was to lose your life in the mines. The workers were being pushed to produce more and more. They were desperate to mine as much ore as possible, as quickly as possible. When a clog developed in a drop shaft,[48] the manager, Hong-Sup Han, decided to use explosives to clear it. But the charge was too big for such a small space, and almost all the workers in that section of the mine were overcome by fumes from the blast. We put together a daring rescue team, and risking life and limb we managed to save a few of the victims. Unfortunately, over twenty workers suffocated before we

---

[47] See Chapter 37, "Stories," for details.

[48] A *drop shaft* is a vertical mineshaft used to drop ore from a higher level to a lower level, where the ore is loaded into waiting minecarts and transported out of the mine.

could get to them, and many more were injured in the tragic accident. Helicopters were sent by the central offices to help, but they arrived too late.

This was a scenario I had witnessed countless times over the years. The managers would emphasize production over safety. When production was the first priority, laborers would be overworked, and managers would take foolhardy risks with the lives of the workers. Due to managers' ambition, many lives would be wasted in accidents such as this one.

Those who survived must be in their seventies and eighties by now. In my case, I was able to retire safely after escaping the most punishing physical work by becoming a surveyor. My survey work involved risk because the intricate and complex calculations contained many pitfalls, but I was lucky to reach retirement age without making any serious mistakes.[49]

Dong-Am required far more work than Kumduck, so there were many occasions when I did not have enough time to take care of my family, and my wife had to keep the house in order on her own. She brought up the two kids, tended to our goat, and cut trees in the hills for firewood. I was often grateful to her, and at the same time sorry for her. Now I regret that I never told her how I felt about her.[50]

Every time I would meet one of my old co-workers at Kumduck, I would hear many sad stories—how one worker had died in an accident in the mines, or how another was suffering from an occupational illness. They toiled all their lives in the mines while holding on to the distant dream that one day they would be brought home. But before they knew it, they got old, and one by one, they passed away. All their suffering had been in vain.

There is a Korean saying that goes, "Over ten years, even the mountains and rivers change." But the mountains and rivers have changed five times, and still some fifty years later there has been no solution to the prisoner-of-war problem. Now many old, tired prisoners who struggled so much are dying. Even today, somewhere in North Korea, these unjust deaths continue.

---

[49] Even one error could result in demotion or a prison sentence.

[50] The patriarch of the traditional Korean family was reserved at home, seldom expressing himself to his wife and children. This did not necessarily mean that fathers like these were unloving or unemotional. They were simply "men of few words" by virtue of culture and upbringing.

My greatest regret was my failure to help my sister Myung-Sook and my brothers Young-Nam and Young-Chul, all of whom had long since moved out and started their own families. I tried to visit them every time I had a break. Whenever I saw them, I felt I had let them down.

While they were growing up, my wife took great care of them, as if they were her own children. We did not have any kids of our own, and did not adopt any children until all of my siblings were married and living on their own. My wife did everything she could for my sister and my brothers. We did manage to send them to school, but in the end they were limited to mine jobs as well. After graduating technical school, Young-Nam and Young-Chul both worked at the nearby No-Un Mine. Myung-Sook worked as an ore dresser at Kumduck.

My three siblings were earnest and model workers. However, my POW status began to hurt them as well. My brothers were not accepted into the Army when they tried to join, even though military service was compulsory in North Korea for most citizens. Military life was tough, but it offered the best opportunity to be admitted to the Party. However, children and close relatives of POWs, as well as others with "complicated" backgrounds, were excluded from military service.

When Young-Nam, Young-Chul, and Myung-Sook were old enough to get married, I tried to find them good spouses from families with respectable political status. However, the only people who were willing to marry them were from families with political classifications similar to our own. Again, it was my status that interfered with the happiness of my siblings.

My sister and my brothers worked hard for their families and even earned service medals, but because of my past, they were never admitted to the Party, no matter how hard they worked. The fact that I, their elder brother, had been an enemy soldier was enough to keep them out.

Sometimes I felt as though my brothers Young-Chul and Young-Nam resented me and thought that it was my fault that they could not succeed. It seemed as though even their wives were beginning to blame me for keeping their husbands from being admitted to the Party.

It hurt to suffer discrimination myself, but to see my sister and my brothers suffer unfair treatment was more painful. It was *I* who had been the enemy soldier, not them, so why were they being punished! Had even one of them been admitted to the Party, I would have been so much less resentful.

Regardless of the circumstances, I had failed to do my duty as their elder brother. To this day, I wonder if there was anything I could have done differently for them. The guilt and the regret continues to haunt me.

24

Starvation

I continued to live in Dong-Am for ten years after retirement. For the first few years, I got extra rations from the government, but as the economy worsened, food became scarce and life got a lot more difficult.[51]

The most pressing need for all ordinary North Koreans was food. Many worried about food on a daily basis, but North Koreans seeking to retire had a special set of concerns. Normal retirees received only 300 grams[52] of rice per day from the government. However, there was a way for a retiree to increase his or her rations.

Since the 1960s, laws had given special treatment to "persons of merit" who earned workers' medals. These people would get better rations after they retired. The law specified four levels of achievement based on the number and degree of medals earned. First and second-level "persons of merit" were allowed 600 grams of rice—twice the normal ration. Thus it was very important for the workers to earn enough awards to break the 600-gram mark. In fact, people hoping to retire sometimes greeted each other by saying, "So, have you reached six hundred yet?"

Most laborers toiled their entire lives for the government and never got a single reward. It was even rarer for a skilled laborer or technician to

---

[51] Chapter 27, "What Went Wrong in North Korea?", offers the author's opinion as to why the economy worsened.

[52] About one and a half cups of rice.

be awarded a medal. While working as a surveyor, I had failed to earn any major awards, such as Party membership, but I had received six smaller medals in recognition of my hard work. These six medals ended up helping me get extra rations. I reached the "600 grams of rice" mark, and also received 56 won[53] per month as a pension, a generous amount relative to most pensions.

But it did not last long. As food became scarce, I no longer got the promised 600 grams a day. The economy itself also declined, so there was a shortage of household necessities.

In North Korea, all household goods, food, fruits, and vegetables were sold at the government-mandated price. Also, wages were set based on the prices for goods. This system worked as long as the government stores had the supply to match the demand of the people. But most of the time, it was impossible to buy goods at the government prices because the government stores did not have enough stock.

The only alternative was the black market, but everything there was too expensive to buy anyway. For example, the government-mandated price for a one-kilogram bag of rice was eight jun[54] but the black market price was eighty won—*a thousand-fold increase*. On the black market, a pair of sneakers that cost five won at a government store would cost one hundred won; an egg that cost seventeen jun at a government store would cost five to six *won*, roughly a thirty-fold increase.

My pension of 56 won per month was a lot compared to others, but 56 won could not even buy one kilo of rice on the black market. It was not enough to survive. In contrast, Party members and those who had connections with government store employees could get special access to goods at government prices. It was inevitable that the living standards of Party members and ordinary people should drift miles apart.

The government stores became known as "Party-member stores" because everyone knew that only Party members could purchase goods there. The rest of us had to rely on the black market, where goods that leaked out the back door of Party-member stores were sold. But more than just illicit goods were for sale. People began to grow their own crops in secret farms and use the food to barter on the black market. Food was

---

[53] North Korean currency. In 2012, the exchange rate was 133,793 won for one US dollar.

[54] *Won* and *jun* are comparable to dollars and cents: 1 won = 100 jun.

worth far more than money itself. It was so valuable that it became the universal currency.

As the system began to break down, people began resorting to bribery and all manner of illicit activity. Eventually corruption became routine and commonplace. Doctors took bribes to write fake notes excusing someone from work. Train conductors sold tickets to scalpers. Laborers bribed officials in order to be assigned to less strenuous work. Party members took bribes from people trying to be inducted. They even took sexual "favors" from young women who sought membership. Everyone was abusing whatever power they had. A common joke was, "Party members cheat proudly, the safety officials cheat safely, and the secret police cheat secretly."

Food was so scarce that every department or organization in the government needed to run its own farms. The Army, the Party, the secret police, the Ministry of Public Safety[55]—all could use their authority to illegally force people to work on these farms. Their natural prey—the desperate individuals who stole food or worked at a black market—was abundant. When the police caught such people, they sent them to work on one of the farms or forced them to collect firewood for the families of the police, without pay. People could be held in bondage for months. Their families, which were already burdened by the loss of a main provider, would then have to use whatever resources they had left to bribe the police to release their captive relative. By taking bribes and exploiting people, the police managed to live well while the rest of the country starved. But mine workers and farmers could not do this; there was nobody below them to victimize.

Up until the '80s, there was still enough food to get by, but in the '90s, catastrophic food shortages began to take place. People who relied solely on government food distribution channels had trouble getting even one meal a day. Those who had no way to get more food could only sit and starve.

Even the Army struggled. Many soldiers had to be sent home to recover from malnourishment. Villagers and farmers who lived near army bases had even more trouble. Soldiers would poach farm animals and strip all the fruit from the orchards. When the Army stole food from either individuals or from the collective farms, the theft went unreported, simply

---

[55] The "Ministry of Public Safety" is the formal term for the North Korean police, as opposed to the secret police, formally known as the "State Security Department."

because no one would dare investigate the Army. "What's the problem with the People's Army taking some of the people's food?" was a sarcastic saying.

The food supply had not completely run out, but most people got less than half their normal rations. Government officials and people whose jobs brought in foreign currency for the government got the highest priority in the supply chain. After them came train conductors, teachers, and doctors, but even these people only got half of their regular rations. Furthermore, their rations were no longer adjusted to account for dependent family members. Those at the lowest end of the food distribution system had their rations stripped away altogether.

Even the victims of the food shortages did not realize the gravity of the situation. "If we can just survive for a few more days," we thought, "they will send us food. How could the government just abandon its people?" So we hung by a thread, subsisting on roots and bark. But no one could last long this way. I watched my neighbors starve to death. It was horrible, and I did not believe I could survive much longer myself.

There were a few things that helped us scrape by during the food shortage. Thankfully, Jung-Mi and Jung-Ho had grown up and could take care of themselves. My wife found part-time work at a farm, so she managed to bring home enough corn to make gruel. I also had a secret farm in the hillside where I grew crops and feed for the goat. It was hard for me to do such labor when my body was so old and weak from years of work in the mines. The work was also very unrewarding, since it was nearly impossible to get a fruitful harvest on the poor land without fertilizer. It was dangerous too—secret farms were highly illegal[56]—but I had no choice.

The economy continued to worsen. Eventually the government stopped providing heating coal, and we had to forage for firewood ourselves. In a region where temperatures regularly dropped to -30°C (-22°F), keeping the house warm was a matter of life and death.

One would think that the government would leave the retired folk alone and allow them to tend to their farms and collect firewood in peace. Instead, they forced everyone, even the elderly, to participate in indoc-trination classes. The slogan was, "Revolutionaries must attend political

---

[56] Despite the food shortages, any enterprise not sponsored by the government, including a private farm, was illegal.

classes until they die!" For many, this was not an empty rallying cry, but a literal prophecy of doom. Between the ideology classes and political assemblies, we did not have time to fight for our survival.

In 1990, people began starving to death. Getting food on a day-to-day basis became an enormous struggle. Sometimes we did not eat for an entire day. When I had been a skilled worker, they had taken advantage of me, but now that I was old and starving, the government did not care whether I lived or died. In 1996 and 1997, I was so malnourished that I did not have the energy to walk around. My neighbors thought that I was going to starve to death soon.

It was rumored that somewhere between two and three million North Koreans starved to death during the food shortage. Several of my friends were among those who died, including Jae-Ul Park, Oon Kim, and Jae-Jun Kim.

25

Emptiness

Though we struggled to survive, my wife and I could not escape the effects of the famine. My wife, who had worked so hard for our family without complaint, gradually got weaker and weaker, and then became gravely ill from what I assumed to be a combination of tuberculosis and malnutrition. She had raised my sister Myung-Sook, my brothers Young-Nam and Young-Chul, and our two adopted children, Jung-Mi and Jung-Ho, and now she needed me. I was not going to let her down.

I took her to the hospital, but the hospital didn't have enough medicine for all of the sick. People with some degree of authority or power were given "emergency medicine," but regular civilians were told to acquire medicine on their own. We tried various folk remedies, but to no avail. No matter what we tried, the sad truth was that we did not have the money to get her good food, let alone proper treatment. It tore at my heart.

I didn't want to ask my siblings for help; they were struggling to survive themselves. I had tried to set up my family members for success by sending them to schools for higher education or to serve in the Army. But due to my POW past, they had been denied advancement. I had worked so hard in hopes of earning equal treatment in North Korean society, but as far as the government was concerned, a former enemy soldier like me was an enemy of the state—forever. Over time, my brothers and sisters, and even my children, resented my status. Looking back, I feel deeply sorry for my children. I often wonder if adopting them was a mistake; their lives were made so difficult because of me.

In the winter of 1993, my wife's sickness got so bad that I had no choice but to write a desperate letter to my brother Young-Chul, begging him to help me take care of my wife. Now in his late forties, he had been medically released from the Kumduck Mine and was with his wife's family, doing light work at a medicinal herb farm. He seemed to be the only one who could help us.

With Young-Chul's agreement, I took Song-Un to his house on December 8 of the same year. I left her there with a promise that I would return in a month to pick her up and bring her home. When I returned to Dong-Am on January 15, 1994, I discovered that the unthinkable had happened.

While I was gone, a fire had destroyed my house, along with the rest of the four-family complex. The fire had started on straw that I had used to feed the goat, and the wind was so strong that my house had burned down in minutes. Some neighbors said that someone had set fire to the feed in order to steal the goat. Regardless of how the house burned down, I thought that this was surely the end for both of us. My house and everything I owned had been burned to ashes. Some neighborhood boys had tried to salvage my portrait of Kim Il-Sung—out of all the things I owned—because they had been taught that it was sacred, but not even that could be saved. I was now homeless—I had nothing more than the clothes on my back. To make matters worse, it was midwinter, and now I did not have a single blanket or any food.

However, thanks to my neighbors and my sister Myung-Sook, I made it through the winter. I felt that I had to survive—so that my poor wife could come back home, if for no other reason. Luckily, since my home was part of a government-owned complex, they began reconstruction at once and finished rebuilding it in only two months. I walked through the front door with nothing but the clothes I was wearing.

As soon as the house was ready, I made the trip to Young-Chul's house in the company of my son, Jung-Ho, who was now in his twenties. I had promised to return for Song-Un in a month, but it had taken two because of the fire that destroyed the house. Jung-Ho and I took turns carrying her all the way to Dong-Am. She was so frail and thin that she felt like nothing more than a piece of paper on my back, and I cried tears of blood[57] with every step at the pain she felt and the terrible injustice of her suffering.

---

[57] "Tears of blood"— 피눈물 —is an idiomatic expression for the overwhelming sorrow one feels when a loved one suffers unjustly. See *Introduction.*

Song-Un's illness had gotten much worse, and I knew she did not have much time left. Desperately, I implored my former bosses—the mining officials and Party representatives—for assistance, *any* assistance, even a blanket. But they were indifferent. They didn't even respond to my requests for help. Maybe I had worked in the mines for decades, but I was still a POW, so they didn't care what happened to me.

This was when I knew for sure that I could not live in North Korea. In the past, I had believed that despite all the trials I had faced, if I worked hard, one day my dedication would be rewarded. So I had done just that and had allowed myself to be exploited, day in, day out, year after year. And here, at last, was the final reward: Now that I was old and useless, nobody gave a damn about me.

My neighbors all thought that both Song-Un and I would pass away soon. But it was too great an injustice to die like this. We were going to survive this ordeal. I considered this a test, and I was determined to pass it.

I did everything I could to get Song-Un admitted to Dong-Am Hospital. Finally, I succeeded, but owing to supply shortages, they had no medicine, so there was little they could do for her. If somehow I were to buy medicine on my own through the black market, the doctors and nurses at the hospital could administer it for me, but it was all moot, because I could not afford black market prices. In fact, the hospital was so bad that I had to cut my own firewood to keep the room warm. Staying at the hospital just made us even more depressed, so I took her back home and had her lie down in our house. It might not have been much, but at least it was ours.

My wife's illness worsened day by day. I was now certain that she was going to pass away soon. There was nothing I could do except cry for her, alone. But even then, my wife was worried about me and tried to comfort me.

One morning, as I was getting dressed to leave, Song-Un called to me. "Honey…" There was no strength left in her voice at all. She forced a smile for me. "I'm sorry I'm causing you so much trouble," she said.

I could barely hold back the tears. "Compared to your suffering, mine is nothing. You'll get better, I know it," I told her. I sat next to her and held her hand. She was so thin her hand felt like a frail tree branch.

"I need to go out, but I will be back soon. Get some rest while I'm gone," I said.

I wanted to tell her that I would return with some delicious food. I wanted to tell her that when she recovered we would go and buy some nice clothes for her. But there was no point in making such empty promises, because we both knew that I did not have the money for such things. I opened the door and turned to look back at her one more time. My heart was torn, but what could I say? I quickly closed the door behind me and wept in silence.

The next morning, on March 14, 1994, my wife laid her head on my lap and quietly passed away. It felt like the sky had fallen and my heart had stopped. In my age and poverty, seeing my ever-supportive wife die before me told me that I would soon follow her.

The funeral was simple. My friends and neighbors, at least, were there to support me. We buried her on the hillside behind my house, which had always been a private spot where we could go just to spend time together. I went to see her grave every day—it was the least I could do for my poor wife. Even now, I pray she rests in peace.

I still remember what my wife said just before she died. As if it were her last will, she told me that I had to survive, to live until reunification, so I could see my father and my sister Gyung-Eh again.[58]

---

[58] Reunification was a kind of "promised land" for most POWs. It was a common wish for there to be some way to go home to see their friends and family in the South.

106

26

The Death of Kim Il-Sung

After Song-Un died, I sat alone in my empty house thinking about what to do with my life. I was sixty-four years old and alone. I felt that if I were ever to get sick and lie down, I would never get up again. However, her last words—telling me that I must survive to see my family again—gave me hope and purpose to live on.

I decided to ask my younger sister, Myung-Sook, for corn seeds to plant in the spring. Until then, I could subsist on the roots and vegetables that grew in the hills. As long as I planted the seeds properly, I thought I could manage to survive.

That year, 1994, there were rumors that South Korean President Kim Young-Sam was coming to visit North Korea to speak with Kim Il-Sung. All North Koreans, weary from years of famine and hardship, were excited about the prospect of any sort of change. Though a meeting did not mean that we would re-unify right away, we hoped that it would open the door to peace and reconciliation between the two nations. We all paid close attention to the upcoming summit.

Whenever there was news about a possible thaw in relations between North and South, the South Korean POWs had the highest hopes. We had been waiting patiently for repatriation for over forty years, and now we were all dead or dying. It was inevitable that we survivors would be excited about the meeting. The two leaders were rumored to meet on August 15, 1994. The POWs, who had spent their lives coping with constant suspicion, surveillance, and discrimination, awaited the President's arrival with bated breath.

When there was a momentous political event like this, the secret police would always call in the POWs. We would be interrogated about our political ideology, and the indoctrination classes would be intensified.

That spring was one of the most difficult times of my life. Often there was not enough food to make a single cup of gruel. I was so malnourished that I was dizzy and could not walk straight. Many people died that spring. Although I had planted seeds, they were not ready for harvest yet, so I had almost no food. My friends and neighbors were worried that I would not survive until the summer harvest.

I barely made it through the spring of 1994. Then, on July 9, there was an order for all North Koreans to listen to a radio broadcast. I hoped that it was good news about President Kim Young-Sam's visit.

The actual news was completely unexpected. The broadcast announced that the Great Leader, Kim Il-Sung, had passed away. It was so unexpected that many of us could not believe our ears. The entire nation was in shock. Kim Il-Sung had ruled for forty-six years. We had not even heard that he was sick or ailing—and now, suddenly, he was dead. For many North Koreans, the world was turned upside down.

Since August 15, 1948, when Korea was liberated from the Japanese empire, Kim Il-Sung had been hailed as the hero of the North. He had promised us that one day we would all live comfortably, eating meat-filled soup and white rice in tile-roofed homes.[59] We had believed that he would eventually come through with his promises. Also, most North Koreans had been brainwashed into seeing Kim Il-Sung as a true leader and patriot.

I saw the television news reports of the entire country grieving his death. Some of Kim Il-Sung's most devoted followers wailed over his death for hours. But brainwashed or not, all North Koreans respected and admired him, and we all mourned his death.

The entire country was crying, but not for the same reasons, it seemed to me. Those who benefited from Kim Il-Sung's regime were truly grateful for the special treatment they got, so they were crying genuine tears of sorrow. But they were also not sure what would happen to them now that his regime had ended, so they were also crying tears of worry. On the other

---

[59] These are historic symbols of luxury in Korea.

hand, the common North Koreans regretted that Kim Il-Sung had died without bringing us the comfortable life that he had promised. They were crying tears of disappointment. Finally, prisoners like me were crying because our only hope for repatriation had been crushed by his death. The meeting between President Kim Young-Sam and Kim Il-Sung had to be canceled. In this weary and lonely life, that meeting had offered a glimmer of hope. Now, that hope had evaporated.

Under the slogan, "Kim Il-Sung will be with us forever," the Juche calendar system was created. The new system set the year of Kim Il-Sung's birth, 1912, as Juche 0. That meant that 1994 became Juche 82. On all official documents, the date was posted as Juche year, Western calendar year, month, and day. Kim Il-Sung's birthday, April 15, was renamed "The Day of the Birth of the Sun," comparing the Great Leader to the sun—the light of the world. We were all told to work harder and study harder in memory of him.

However, after Kim Il-Sung's death, life in North Korea became more difficult. Our already meager rations got even smaller, and our wretched lives got more miserable. Many people missed the time when Kim Il-Sung was still alive. There were some people who truly believed that Kim Il-Sung had worked hard to bring us the paradise that he had promised, though there were detractors who said that he was a vain dictator and an impractical isolationist.[60]

After half a century of struggle in North Korea, I had learned that the proletarian paradise promised by Kim Il-Sung was a fantasy and a lie. I had witnessed firsthand the absurdity of the society, and until I was almost seventy, my entire life revolved around hunger and oppression. I was always put down and never able to speak my mind freely.

---

[60] These "detractors" were simply ordinary people who voiced frustration with the regime, not public figures speaking openly or publishing their beliefs.

27

What Went Wrong in North Korea?

How did North Korea become so poor? Even though North Koreans are every bit as hardworking and responsible as their South Korean brothers, the North suffers from chronic hunger and starvation, while the South prospers. After many years of living in North Korea, I have formed some opinions as to why this is so.

First of all, the government wasted too much money and effort worshipping Kim Il-Sung and his son Kim Jong-Il. The lavish and expensive structures built throughout the country, such as Juche research centers or monuments to Kim Il-Sung and Kim Jong-Il, consumed massive amounts of resources that might otherwise have been used to construct schools, homes, or hospitals for the people. Towns and cities compete to build the best monuments, and these monuments are at the center of every school, from nursery school to college. Propaganda is everywhere. Even in the remote countryside, money is spent to carve quotes from Kim Il-Sung into the sides of cliffs. On top of this, an expensive memorial or plaque is built to honor every place Kim Jong-Il or Kim Il-Sung have ever visited, everything they have done, and everything they have said. The entire country is devoted to worshipping them. Even as the citizens are starving, money is wasted on these useless tributes.

Second, the government built too many factories and facilities. Ambitious officials took Kim Il-Sung's Juche ideal of self-reliance too far. These bootlickers built shoe factories, soap factories, textile mills, and other factories in every city and village in order to impress him. But today these factories do not produce anything because they don't have enough raw materials. They just sit, idly collecting dust. The factory workers are required to show up every day, but they don't have any work to do. So even though the country is dotted with shoe factories, many citizens worry about getting proper shoes. A few central factories would have been more efficient and adequate for the entire country.

This happened even at Dong-Am,[61] where there were several small, barely operational factories. When these factories *did* produce anything, it was always of poor quality: light bulbs, for instance, that only worked for a few days, or shoes that wore out quickly. We came to rely on Chinese goods, which were of comparatively high quality. We needed matches to set fire to wood—our main source of fuel—but the North Korean factories couldn't even make good matches, so we had to use more expensive Chinese gas lighters.

Food production had similar problems. There were farms for all sorts of animals—ducks, chickens, pigs, and even rabbits—but none of the farms got enough feed for the animals, so they were all empty.

Lastly, many problems were caused by Kim Jong-Il and his "military-first" policy. In order to consolidate his influence with the generals after the death of his father in 1994, he pandered to them and invested heavily in the armed forces. Though North Korea had always been a militaristic nation, it got much worse once Kim Jong-Il took over. For example, every farmer was required to raise one pig, or at least a goat, a year for the army. This might not sound like much, but in a country where farmers had trouble feeding themselves, it was almost impossible for them to feed a pig that they would never get to eat. It was a huge tax, but it was the only way the government could feed its one-million-man army and pander to the officers.

The government also needed foreign currency, but since the country didn't produce any goods worth exporting, the government forced the people to bring in exportable materials. There were set quotas that each person had to meet. For instance, schoolchildren each had to bring in two high-quality rabbit skins per year, and rural wives had to "donate" castor oil, silkworms, or medicinal plants and herbs to the state. Retired people were no exception; they were ordered to pan for gold and collect medicinal herbs. These items would be exported to earn foreign currency that the

---

[61] Dong-Am was a tiny mining town in the middle of the mountains, far from any population centers, so it is surprising that any factories were built there at all.

government desperately needed. Those who failed to meet their quotas were harassed for being disloyal to the country and the Party.

These quotas for exportable goods were also imposed upon organizations within North Korea, including companies, and even the Army itself. This led to ridiculous behavior. In order to fulfill their quota, companies would assign a few employees to bring in the company quota of exportable materials instead of doing their real job. The Army would assign units or platoons to work in mines or do other labor that earned the exportable material.

It did not matter how absurd the process was. We were all afraid of being criticized and punished, so we had to do what we were told to do. The way we collected exportable material reflected the problems in the economy as a whole. No matter how ridiculous and inefficient the system was, nobody dared to bring up any problems, because they would be punished. This ensured that the broken system could never be repaired. Thus the efforts of the hardworking and responsible people of North Korea were squandered at every stage.

28

Mortal Struggle

Following the death of my wife, I felt like I had no sense of purpose, no hope that made life worth living. Although I worked hard, life was very difficult. I did what I could do to survive. I fetched firewood and cultivated the soil, but it was too much for me. I was alone, weak, and had nothing but my bare hands. I did not know how much longer I could continue to hang on.

The famine grew much worse.[62] In order to survive, the people of Dong-Am ate any plant that was not poisonous. Still, many starved to death. I witnessed many of my friends die this way. I couldn't list all the countless people I knew who died of starvation. There were rumors that some people even resorted to cannibalism.

Over time, my siblings, Young-Nam, Young-Chul, and Myung-Sook, could not help me. They had long since left my home, and they had problems of their own. I once went to my younger sister Myung-Sook's house to beg for some food, but my brother-in-law turned me away, yelling at me that I was a drain on their family. "You've lived to seventy—you don't need to live much more!" he said.

Another time, my son, Jung-Ho, came over to visit me. Jung-Ho had been living in the mine dormitories, and when he saw the condition I was in, he tried to help me. He went to my brother Young-Nam's house to beg

---

[62] It is estimated that between 600,000 and 3 million people—3% to 15% of the population—died of starvation during the famines of the mid-1990s.

for some potato scraps, but my sister-in-law kicked him out, yelling, "You son-of-a-bitch! Nobody has any food around here. Don't come to us!"

But even in the worst of times, there were still some generous and caring people who kept me alive. These were not my relatives, but my friends and neighbors.

One of these friends was Dae-Sung Kang. He was a fellow prisoner of war, and we had worked together at both the Kumduck and Dong-Am mines, so we were very close. One day, I showed up at his house, penniless and shameless, to beg for food. His wife made me the most delicious meal, and even gave me a few cups of corn to take home. This tiny bit of food saved my life. I am forever indebted to Kang.[63]

Another friend who helped me was Myung-Su Kim, my neighbor. He used to be a member of the *Chochongryon*—the pro-North Korean faction in Japan. He came to North Korea voluntarily and became a high-ranking Party member until his fall from grace.[64] After several years at the Yodok Penal Labor Camp, he was released to Dong-Am, where he had to work as a mine laborer. Myung-Su was a skilled organizer. After he retired from labor, he put together communal farms where local elderly folk could work part-time. I will never forget the impact he had on my life.

So it was that I barely managed to scrape out a living. Old, lonely, isolated, and destitute, I watched the final years of the twentieth century pass by.

Even in this desperate situation, we found a faint promise of freedom. We began hearing rumors about some daring people who were crossing the border into China to smuggle goods. The smugglers, mostly young women,[65] would have to bribe the border guards and soldiers. If they got caught, they would be severely punished, but it was better than starving to death.[66] The North Korean border was starting to break down.

---

[63] Kang escaped to South Korea one month before the author.

[64] In the cutthroat North Korean society, where the easiest way to get promoted is to inform on others and implicate them in political crimes, it is fairly common for higher-ups to suddenly fall out of favor and get sent to political prison camps or penal labor camps.

[65] North Korean men were all required to show up to work, even if there was no work to be done, and there were severe consequences for anyone who was absent. Women were the only people who had time not accounted for by the government. Once the government food distribution stopped, it was women who tended the secret fields or worked at black markets to feed their families while their husbands were stuck at their jobs. Consequently, women became the first to engage in any unauthorized activity, including smuggling.

[66] Travel within North Korea is severely restricted. Permits are required even to leave town. Travel outside the country is strictly forbidden and punishable by death.

The news that people were traveling outside the country gave me a reason to cling to life. After paying close attention to any news or information regarding China, I learned that South Koreans were traveling freely in and out of China.[67] This meant that if I could escape to China, I might be able to make it back home.

---

[67] While it may seem obvious to anyone else that people regularly travel between China and South Korea, a North Korean would find this shocking. The North Korean government constantly reminds the citizens of the state of war between North and South Korea, and since China is North Korea's closest ally, it would be difficult for a North Korean to believe that China allows South Koreans to travel freely between the two countries.

29

Summit

As I languished hopelessly in Dong-Am, exciting and unexpected news came in May of 2000. The South Korean president, Kim Dae-Jung, stated that he would make a visit to North Korea and meet with Chairman Kim Jong-Il, the successor to Kim Il-Sung. If such a meeting occurred, it would be a landmark event. The previous North-South Summit had been canceled upon the unexpected death of Kim Il-Sung.[68] We hoped that this time the talks would lead to a more peaceful and friendly relationship between the two countries and allow the borders to reopen.

Indeed there were signs that relations were improving. For example, there was the South Korean *chaebol*, Jung Joo-Young,[69] who brought 1000 cows across the DMZ to North Korea. Jung was born in territory that is now inside North Korea, but had gone to the South prior to the war. Even though he was a capitalist, Jung Joo-Young was hailed as a hero in the North by both the government and the people. He was viewed as a prodigal son of sorts who had made a fortune in the South but had never forgotten his Northern brothers.

But now the President himself was coming to visit. This captivated every North Korean. All we talked about was what this visit would come to mean. *Why is he coming? What does he hope to accomplish? What kind*

---

[68] See Chapter 26, "The Death of Kim Il-Sung"

[69] Jung Joo-Young (1915 – 2001) was the founder and Chairman of the Hyundai Group, a massive South Korean conglomerate involved in industries from shipbuilding to auto manufacturing. The term *chaebol* refers to these conglomerates or their owners.

of welcoming ceremony will there be? We speculated endlessly about the visit. Some people said that just as the weak come to pay their respects to the strong, Kim Dae-Jung was coming to visit Kim Jong-Il. Others were sure that he was coming here on the advice of Jung Joo-Young.

Personally, I wondered how the visiting president would be welcomed, since only weeks ago the government had been criticizing him as an American puppet. During his time as the leader of the minority party in the South, there had once been a newspaper article complimenting him as a pro-democracy activist. But as soon as he became President, he of course received nothing but criticism from the North Korean press.

After the official announcement of Kim Dae-Jung's visit was made public, the government began increasing the emphasis on political indoctrination by ordering extra political classes to be held. At the classes, they warned us not to get our hopes up and to remain vigilant against the South.

Nothing, however, could dampen the mood. This would be the first such meeting since the end of the war. The North Koreans had suffered for many years, so they were desperate for some change. Of course we prisoners, who had been oppressed and exploited for as long as we could remember, were even more anxious. Though we dared not hope to be fully and officially repatriated, we could at least go home, if only the two countries would open their borders to each other.

This was my very last hope. I waited anxiously for *my* president's visit. Everyone in the mines and everyone in North Korea hoped for an improvement in the situation.

On June 13, 2000, President Kim Dae-Jung arrived in North Korea. I really wanted to watch the landing and the arrival, so I traveled to a house that had a color TV. Though there were a few black-and-white TVs in my village, I wanted to watch it in full color. When I got to the house, it was already packed, so I begged to be let in.

I watched as the President and the First Lady stepped down from the plane. Then, in a moving scene, the President warmly shook hands with Kim Jong-Il. I did not realize it at first, but I was tearing up. I stared intently at the screen, my heart brimming with hope.

The President was welcomed by a crowd of Pyongyang residents holding flowers. I think that the joy on the people's faces was genuine. Since becoming independent from Japan, the two sides had been locked in an ideological battle that started the Korean War and claimed countless lives on both sides. Even after the ceasefire, there was constant strife between the two nations. But seeing the two leaders greet each other so warmly could bring anyone to tears.

Though we knew that there were innumerable issues to be resolved at the summit conference, we prayed that our leaders would not forget the problem of the South Korean POWs. I felt more than ever that my struggle here in the North was bound to end, one way or the other.

After a few days, the June 15th Joint Statement was declared. From the declaration, it seemed that relations between the two sides would indeed improve. To the South Korean POWs, however, it was an indescribable letdown, because there was not even a single mention of the POWs in the statement or in any other report. It seemed as if Kim Dae-Jung had not even brought up the issue. Perhaps we had hoped for too much, but now we were devastated. There was not even a hint of our plight in the statement.

Have they truly forgotten about us? How could he ignore us like this? Is this guy really the voice of the South Korean people? Thoughts such as these consumed us.

After the death of my wife, I had suffered six miserable years alone. In all those years, not once had I been able to eat even one full and satisfying meal—not even so much as a bowl of corn gruel. Why was I still alive?

During that time, my younger brother Young-Chul, who had taken my wife into his home when she was sick, passed away. My younger sister Myung-Sook also died of an occupational illness during those years. They had both worked so hard to become Party members, but the hard labor and toxic materials in the mines eventually killed them. I was crushed, and buried each of them in my heart. As their older brother, it was my duty to protect them and help them become successful. Instead, my POW status had held them back. I had let them down.

I was now seventy years old. I was done. I had had enough.

My last wish was to again set foot on my homeland, a free man, before I died. Kim Dae-Jung's visit had only rekindled my desire to go home. I wanted to get out of this hell, even if it cost me my life.

30

Crossroads

Kim Dae-Jung's trip to North Korea was over, and he had left without a single mention of the South Korean POWs. Maybe we had allowed our hopes to get the better of us, but we had really believed that our President cared about us. After he was gone, we felt betrayed. I was so upset that I became physically ill.

When my daughter, Jung-Mi, found out I was sick, she came to visit me with her friend Young-Sung, an attractive lady in her mid-30s. I did not have any food to spare for them at all. In better times, this would have been a happy occasion, but destitute as we were, the visit felt hollow. We were both burdens upon each other.

During their visit, Jung-Mi began asking me specific questions about my past. This seemed to come from out of the blue. In truth, I had never explained to my children that I was a South Korean POW, but Jung-Mi had probably figured it out by now. I decided that there was no point in telling her what she already knew, so I avoided her questions.

Jung-Mi then told me that Young-Sung was one of the daring female smugglers who risked their lives going back and forth across the border with China. This, along with her questioning, convinced me that there was more to her visit than just checking up on me.

A few days later, Young-Sung came by herself. She told me all about China and South Korea. According to her, South Koreans traveled freely to and from China. She then asked me cautiously, "Were you ever a South Korean soldier?"

After thinking a moment, I replied, "You know your father's friend, Chul-Mo Kang? He knows very well about my past. Go ask him." Chul-Mo was a fellow POW and we had known each other for many years.

A few days later, I met Chul-Mo at an indoctrination class. I asked him if he had met with Young-Sung. Indeed, Young-Sung had come to him and spoken with him. He then added that it would be a blessing to "visit" China. This confirmed my suspicions that Young-Sung had something big planned for me. I was not surprised when Young-Sung came again on July 19, roughly a month later, and asked if I would like to escape to China. It was now time for me to decide. On the one hand, I could stay here in this hell. At least it was a hell I was used to. On the other, I could take a big risk and go down a very difficult path in search of a better future.

I was at another crossroads—probably the last one I would encounter in my life. When I closed my eyes, I could see pivotal scenes from my past: the day I was press-ganged into the North Korean Army, my capture by the ROK and the hell of Koje-Do Prison, the day I saw my father again, how I enlisted for the South, and finally the day on the battlefield when I became a POW again in North Korea. These were the moments that had decided my fate.

That evening Young-Sung and I had a long talk. I confessed to her every detail about my past as a South Korean soldier and then a POW. I also revealed my deep desire to somehow make it back to my homeland. Then she told me a story of her own.

She warned me that escaping the country was very difficult, and she could under no circumstances guarantee that I would make it. But if I was willing to take the risk, she was ready to take me at least to China. Since she had crossed the border a few times, she was well-acquainted with the secret routes.

I did not hesitate. I had already made up my mind. Life in North Korea was not a life worth living. I wanted to spend my final years in freedom. I told Young-Sung that I wanted to go with her.

"You realize," she warned, "If we get caught, we're dead."

"Yeah, I know. But I'm as good as dead here anyway," I said. "I'm ready to risk my life to get out of here."

During the war, I had survived bombs and bullets. I was aware that this journey would be even more dangerous. But I was prepared to face the risk and be free, or die trying. Those were my only two options.

"All right, then get ready, because we are leaving tomorrow," she said.

With that, Young-Sung crept away from my house under cover of darkness. As she left, I sighed deeply. I had just made a decision that would—one way or another—permanently alter the course of my remaining life. Tomorrow I would embark on a journey that would either take me to freedom or get me killed.

That evening I had trouble sleeping.

"*How ironic*," I thought. "*A little more than a month ago, there was a historic summit between the North and South to talk about peace and reconciliation. We POWs had waited fifty years for this meeting, yet nothing happened as a result of it. Nobody is coming for me. Now here I am, trying to find some way to go home on my own. I've got to make it home alive*," I decided. "*Someone has to tell the story of the South Korean Prisoners of War.*"

31

Escape

Before I knew it, morning came. It was July 20, 2000. That day, the elderly and the housewives of Dong-Am were scheduled to clean up a footpath on a nearby hill. I would need an excuse to leave, since Young-Sung and I planned to meet at noon at the Dong-Am Train Station.

In order to avoid suspicion, I went to work cleaning up the footpath in the morning, as I was supposed to do. Luckily my daughter, Jung-Mi, was staying over. Before I went to work, I told her to come to where I was working at around 11:00 and call me loudly.

Right on time, she came over and yelled, "Father! The herbal medicine doctor has come to check up on you. Why don't you come down for a minute?"

Most of the people in the village knew of my bad health, so they did not take particular notice of this. I went to the work-crew manager and asked to leave for the doctor. I told him I would return to work as soon as I could. In order to make it seem like I was going to come back soon, I left my tools at the worksite and hurried home.

At home I found a small meal that Jung-Mi had prepared for me to eat before I left. After eating the plate of ground corn, I went to the train station to meet Young-Sung. I didn't say goodbye to Jung-Mi. I had told her that I was just going to China with Young-Sung to get some medicine, and that I'd be coming back. For Jung-Mi's safety, I had to keep the real plan to myself. If she knew, and I got caught, she would get in trouble for helping me escape the country.

At the Dong-Am Station, I met up with Young-Sung and her twelve-year-old daughter, Mok-Ran. Young-Sung had decided that this would be her last trip to China. She was fleeing to the South with her daughter.

Escaping with us to China was Min-Shik Kang and his seven-year-old daughter, Soon-He—five people in all. Min-Shik Kang was the son of my friend Chul-Mo Kang, whom Young-Sung had taken to China ten days ago. Chul-Mo had asked Young-Sung to take Min-Shik and his young daughter across the border, too. It might seem dangerous to bring two young children on a trip like this, but having two kids along would help us avoid suspicion. The five of us could pretend to be a family. I would be the elderly grandfather, while Min-Shik and Young-Sung would look like a father and a mother with two young daughters in tow.

We traveled for a few days and arrived at the port city of T'anchon. Now came the difficult part of our journey. We needed travel papers to buy tickets to Chongjin[70] and to pass the routine inspections. But Young-Sung was the only person in our group with travel papers. We needed her people skills to get tickets for the rest of us.

The T'anchon Station was crowded. Many people were waiting for the Chongjin-bound train, which was running late. They all looked tired and hungry. Some of them, including soldiers and policemen, had missed meals while waiting for the train.

Young-Sung knew she could exploit this. She carefully approached three policemen and quickly befriended them. Once she figured out that they were very hungry, she went to a nearby black market and bought cold beer and lots of food. She invited the policemen to sit down and eat with us.

Even policemen do not have enough money to eat well while they travel, so they gratefully joined our meal. While we were eating, Young-Sung flirted with the three of them. She was exceedingly pretty, and at 5'3" she was fairly tall for a North Korean woman. Once she had won them over, she casually asked for a favor.

---

[70] Chongjin is a major port city and provincial capital of North Hamgyong Province. It is also a transportation hub.

"We had to leave quickly, so my husband and my father didn't have time to get travel papers. We already got our tickets on the black market, but we need papers to pass the inspection. Do you think you could help us out somehow?" She asked.

These policemen had enough clout to get us through the line with ease. In a good mood from the food and drinks, they told her not to worry. When the train arrived, the policemen accompanied us to the ticket inspector[71] and told the inspector that we were "family." That was enough to get us through.

Once we were on the train, the policemen suggested that we stay in the luggage cars to avoid the passenger inspections. We followed their advice. In the luggage cars, there were a few people lying down here and there— mostly other illicit travelers like us.

At the Chongjin Station, Young-Sung used the same tricks she had used at T'anchon to get us onto the Musan-bound train. Musan was a border town, so the travel inspections there were very rigorous. Young-Sung knew this, so instead of getting off at the Musan Station, we got off at a much smaller station just before Musan.

At the smaller station, a few people got on or off and there was not even a single inspection agent. But this station was far from Musan. We walked for a long time, until we managed to stop a passing truck. We bribed the driver with good food and expensive cigarettes to let us hitchhike with him, and he took us safely to Musan.

At Musan, we stayed with a friend of Young-Sung's and planned the most dangerous part of the journey: getting to the border.[72]

I looked very much like a sick patient traveling to see a doctor. I was wearing shabby clothes, and I was so tired that I was on the verge of collapse. Young-Sung decided to use my sick appearance to our advantage. She told me to act deaf and unresponsive from my sickness.

We hoped to reach Young-Sung's friend's house in the Sambong area. Her friend's house was very close to the Tumen River, which is the border between North Korea and China. The road to Sambong was long

---

[71] The ticket inspector makes sure the person getting on the train has the right ticket and travel papers.

[72] Just getting to the border is more dangerous than the crossing itself. There are many checkpoints on the road north, and all the residents of these border towns are encouraged to act as informants and report any suspicious travelers.

and filled with travel checkpoints. Our plan was to pretend to be a Musan family heading north to a friend's house in Sambong to pick up herbs and medicine for me, the sick old grandpa.

In order to disguise myself as a Musan resident, Young-Sung brought me a borrowed ID from someone my age living in Musan. Though there was a photo on the ID card, the inspectors usually focused more on making sure the address was correct. I took the hand of Young-Sung's twelve-year-old daughter, while Min-Shik held his seven-year-old daughter, and the five of us walked to Sambong as if we were on a casual family trip.

Along the way, there were many travel checkpoints. Since I was so old, the inspectors rarely checked me, but Min-Shik was checked often because he was a young man. Several times we came close to getting caught, but every time Young-Sung saved us with her bribes and her charm. For bribes, we gave the inspectors liquor, cigarettes, and some dried squid snacks.[73] The bribes helped a little, but what really got us past the inspectors were Young-Sung's beauty and her ability to talk her way out of any situation.

We walked all day. It was dusk by the time we neared Young-Sung's friend's house. In this area, everyone, even the children, questioned strangers like a travel inspector. They would interrogate any stranger on where they were going and who they were. Though we were very close to our destination, the danger was greater than ever. I was a nervous wreck, as were the others.

As we approached another border town, Min-Shik got very pale. Finally he cried, "I've had enough of this!"

Min-Shik did not think we could pass through the next town safely, and even if we made it all the way to the Tumen River, he didn't think that he could cross it safely. We tried to convince him otherwise, but he refused to change his mind. I was distraught—*how could he just give up after we had come this far?*

Night was fast approaching, so we didn't have the time to keep talking to him. We had to keep moving. Min-Shik took his daughter, and we parted ways.

Young-Sung, twelve-year-old Mok-Ran, and I kept going, nervously. Every time we passed another stranger, I was filled with dread. When I saw

---

[73] Dried squid is a very popular Korean snack. It is salty and chewy, not unlike beef jerky.

a shadow behind us, my heart skipped a beat. Luckily it was getting dark, so there weren't many people out. I had no luggage, and I was holding hands with Mok-Ran, so we could easily pass for a family coming home from a short trip.

As night fell, we arrived at Young-Sung's friend's house. We were warmly welcomed by an old man. Young-Sung must have told her friend that we were coming. It was July 27, which happened to be the anniversary of the signing of the armistice that called a ceasefire in the Korean War. It had taken seven days to get here from Dong-Am.

Once we were inside, Young-Sung explained that we needed to cross the river that night. She asked her friend for some help in exchange for the last of our "gifts"—beer, cigarettes, dried squid, and quite a lot of cash. Like most North Koreans, Young-Sung's friend was very poor. As the number of travelers and escapees from North Korea had grown, he had begun to scrape out a living by helping people across the Tumen.

He told us to go rest in the kitchen and wait. Once nightfall had truly set in, we could begin planning the final portion of our escape.

I learned that Young-Sung's friend often walked around the river dikes and spied on the movements of the border guards. He was very experienced; he knew when the guards changed shifts and when they were most tired.

We nervously hid out in the kitchen. The fear of getting caught made time pass with agonizing slowness. A minute felt like an hour. Finally, after what felt like an age, the old man called to us. It was three in the morning. We followed Young-Sung's friend out into a cornfield and walked toward the border.

The moon was our only light in the dark field. We did our best to walk quietly, but we could not avoid making slight sounds as we rustled a leaf or stepped on a branch. Every time we heard a noise, we froze. As we finally neared the river, I was drenched in sweat and cramping from the long and tense walk. We crossed over the dike and made it to the waterfront. The river's current was lapping against the shore. Off in the distance we could barely make out the lights on the other side—China.

At last, here we were: the final threshold. As I watched the waves on the river passing by, I was overcome with mixed emotions. Part of me was nervous—crossing the river was going to be tough—but I was also relieved that we had made it this far. Young-Sung's friend used hand signals to point out where the river was the narrowest. Then he waved goodbye and disappeared.

After he left, we waded into the river with our clothes on. I wanted to move quickly, but it was more important to stay silent, so we could advance only one step at a time. Halfway across, the current was very strong, and the slippery rocks made it hard to stay balanced. I felt as if I could be carried away at any moment. We put Young-Sung's daughter in between us, and holding hands, we continued along the river.

The strong current kept us from walking in a straight line. With every step, I was hit with a wave of nausea. I felt like I would collapse at any second. If my legs gave way here, I knew I would never get up again. Using our last reserves of energy, we fought through the current and barely made it to the opposite shore.

On the night of July 27, 2000, I set foot on Chinese soil for the first time. Exhausted, I collapsed on the riverbank and lay there for a while. Once I had caught my breath, I turned around and looked back across the Tumen at the land I had just escaped.

A tear slowly rolled down my cheek. I was overcome with conflicting emotions. In a way, I felt an attachment to the land. It was my birthplace; my dear mother's hometown was there, too. But on the other hand, I was overjoyed to finally be free from that hell. It was a place where I had experienced untold amounts of pain and suffering. I have a very complex relationship with the North indeed.

Young-Sung whispered, "Welcome to China!"

I held her hands in gratitude. This young woman had done for me what my country could not do—free me from North Korea.

32

Escape from China

We had made it to China, but we were still in danger. We still had to worry about the Chinese Public Safety Bureau (PSB). The PSB hunted for North Korean escapees like us by going house to house in villages where many *Joseonjoks*,[74] who were known to hide escapees, lived. We had to keep moving. I followed Young-Sung to a neat-looking house. When Young-Sung knocked on the door, a lady welcomed us with a bright smile. Our clothing was still wet from the river crossing, so she gave us dry clothes that we could change into.

She offered us a room and suggested that we rest awhile. But there was little rest for the weary. Morning came quickly. During the day, the cops would be patrolling the area, so we had to leave quickly. The lady told us to go to her relative's house, so we ate a quick breakfast and took off. The relative lived in a remote village, and we would be a little safer there. But we had to keep moving.[75] We went from house to house, never staying in one place for very long.

---

[74] *Joseonjok* refers to ethnic Koreans living in China, an ethnic group of long standing. There are approximately 850,000 *Joseonjok* living in the Yianban Korean Autonomous Prefecture, which lies on the border between North Korea and China.

[75] If caught by the Chinese PSB, a North Korean escapee would be deported back to the North, where they would be tortured and more than likely executed.

We were approached by many "brokers" offering to help us get in touch with my relatives in South Korea. Brokers make a living by smuggling escaped North Koreans to South Korea—a very lucrative business.[76] Young-Sung could get me from North Korea to China, but she didn't know how to get from China to South Korea, so we simply had to trust these brokers. Hiding out in China was terrifying. We constantly faced the threat of getting caught by the PSB.

Finally a broker came forward who claimed to have contacted my family in South Korea. He told me that my father was still alive, and he had remarried while I was in North Korea. My sister, Gyung-Eh, who had been in the South with my father when the war ended, was alive as well. The broker then said that he could connect me with my stepbrother, who had been born while I was in the North.

His name, he said, was Young-Jin. A few days later, I spoke to Young-Jin on the phone. I can't begin to describe how I felt when I heard his voice. We didn't have long to speak; all we could do was quickly identify each other. After we hung up, I was in a speechless daze. I wasn't sure if this was real or if I was dreaming. Would I be returning to my homeland at last?

In the middle of all this, I was separated from Young-Sung. We had originally planned to go to the South together, but the situation did not allow it. With considerable dismay, we had to part company on the doorstep of success. But we had no choice.

I was so close to freedom, and yet so far. Now that Young-Sung was gone, my fate was entirely in the hands of the brokers. If something went wrong, I could be sent back to North Korea and executed.

---

[76] China has a fairly substantial industry built around smuggling North Korean refugees from China into South Korea. About 3,000 North Koreans defect to South Korea every year, normally with the help of "brokers." These brokers charge about $3,500 to get from North Korea to China and $2,500 to get from China to South Korea. Payment comes in a variety of ways. They might contact South Korean relatives of the escapee and charge an up-front fee, or the escapee might pay back the broker after arriving in South Korea.

With a South Korean prisoner of war, however, the brokers can charge much more. The South Korean government does not directly give out a reward for rescuing the POWs. Instead, it treats the POW as a soldier returning from battle, and gives them back pay with interest. Although the conscripts are not paid much, over fifty years it can add up to quite a lot of money—up to several hundred thousand dollars. Knowing this, the brokers can charge much more to help a POW escape. Thus they give top priority to helping POWs.

A few days later I learned that my stepbrother, Young-Jin, had arrived in China. Then I was taken to a small hotel where I met my brother for the first time.

When he saw me, he shouted, "Is it really you, Young-Bok?"

"Yes, it's me," I replied. "You must be Young-Jin."

We embraced warmly, tears rolling down our cheeks. Meeting my stepbrother for the first time was a little awkward, but after talking awhile, I could tell that he truly was a brother to me.

That evening, we got on an overnight train heading for Shenyang. The brokers had bought us tickets on a flight to Korea that was scheduled to take off from the Shenyang Airport on August 30. We were flying illegally, and it was important not to draw attention to ourselves, so we got to the airport the day before our departure and practiced going through the check-in procedures.

On August 30, 2000, it was finally time for the flight. Young-Jin and I got to the airport, where a big plane awaited us on the runway. I began to walk toward it. Behind me was my stepbrother. *"Just one short trip,"* I thought, *"and I'm going to be back in the South with my family."* It was all so surreal—I couldn't believe it was actually happening. At the same time, I was shaking and nervous; I was sure that someone would notice and arrest me. With bated breath, I finally made it to the plane.

With every step up the ramp stairs, I saw my family members before my eyes. First, I saw my mother and my lovely wife. I was sad that they could not join me in the South. Then came my brother Young-Chul and my sister Myung-Sook, who had passed away in the North. After them, I saw my sister Gyung-Sook, and my younger brother Young-Nam, who were still alive in the North, as well as my children, Jung-Mi and Jung-Ho. I felt guilty that I was leaving them behind to struggle there, but I knew that I could not survive even one more year in that hell. I needed to get out.

At the top of the steps, I glanced back at Young-Jin. He nodded slightly to me. We entered the cabin, strapped ourselves into our seats, and then the plane began to taxi onto the runway. Before I knew it, we had taken off, and we were in the air.

"You can relax now. When we get off the plane, we will be in Korea!" my brother exclaimed.

I used to tell my POW friends that I wouldn't go to the South unless the Peninsula was reunified and my family could come down with me. I told them that they should go to the South first, if they ever tried to repatriate the prisoners. Now here I was, on the way to Korea before them. I felt sorry for my friends, the POWs, who had struggled together with me in the North.

33

Homecoming

As soon as I sank into my seat, I felt all the tension and fear of the past few weeks finally release. Exhausted, I felt my eyes droop shut at once. Like a panorama, I could see the past seventy years of my life. Only two months ago, I had been in the North, lingering close to death. Now, here I was, about to return to the home that I so desperately desired. The memories of my time in the North were fresh, yet distant, as if they were memories from a past life. I think the sense of distance arose because I was traveling to a totally new world.

My heart beat quickly when I thought about my family, the family I would soon be seeing, but I was a little worried as well. How would I be welcomed, now that I was coming back an old cripple? After all, even though I had been dragged to the North as a prisoner, I had spent my entire life serving them. I even remembered my indoctrination lessons about the terrible torture chambers run by the KCIA, where the punishments, they said, drove people insane.

I was lost in thought for a while, and before I knew it we touched down at Gimpo International Airport in South Korea. I looked out the window and saw the beautiful, cloudless sky. It was the same sky I had seen in North Korea, but here in the South it looked completely different.

Inside the Arrivals Lobby, I saw my family waiting for me. There was my aged father, in a wheelchair, surrounded by my stepmother, my sister, and many other relatives. I slowly walked toward them. Overwhelmed by the sight of my family, my mind had long since gone blank—I didn't know what to think.

Finally, I crossed the distance between us, my heart pounding. I couldn't believe this was actually happening. After so many years of waiting and hoping to see my family again, I was speechless now that they were here in front of me. How does one start a conversation with family members one has not seen or heard from in over fifty years? It was as if I were meeting them all for the first time.

I knelt in front of my ninety-four-year-old father and held his hand. "Father, it's me," I said, "Young-Bok. I've made it back..." That was all I could get out before my throat went dry. The feeling of my father's thin, old hand was too much for me. It reminded me of how much time had passed since I had seen him last. I began to sob.

My father stared at me blankly. He didn't recognize me. The last time he had seen me, I was a young man, barely in my twenties. Now I was old, with "white hair". My own father could not recognize me, his son. I was crushed.

My sister Gyung-Eh said, "A long time ago, we got a letter that you'd been killed in battle. He has lived the past fifty years believing you were dead."

I nodded, and slowly began to stand up, when I felt my father's grip tighten on my hand. Our eyes met, and I think I saw something stirring deep within him. Maybe it was just a coincidence, but I'm sure that in that moment he remembered me.

Unfortunately, our reunion had to be cut short. My identity hadn't been officially confirmed. A government official led me to a waiting car, which took me to some designated place in the city to get processed. While I had ridden in busses and trains before, it was the first time I had ridden in a car.[77] I looked out the window at the city. The splendid buildings, the bustling streets, and the sheer number of cars on the road were unbelievable. I had no idea how prosperous and developed the South had become. It looked like a city from the future.

We arrived at some government building and began the identification process. After some initial questions and basic verification, they showed

---

[77] Before the Korean War, private cars were a nearly unattainable luxury, and in the postwar North only ranking Party members have cars of their own. Even in the South, most families did not have cars until the 1990s.

me to a comfortable room. I finally relaxed and spent my first night there. I closed my eyes and tried to take everything in. It took a few hours to recover from the shocking things I had seen that day.

I was a little worried about the upcoming identification process. My situation was a little different from that of most returning POWs. I had roots in the North—my family—so I had worked hard for the North Korean government. My effort had even earned me a few workers' medals. I was afraid that the South might consider that to be treasonous.

The next morning I went to the processing room, where three officials came to interview me. It was intimidating at first, but the officials must have noticed my nervousness, because one of them started off by saying, "We are so glad that you returned to the South, Mr. Yoo. We know you have faced many difficulties in the North, and on behalf of the country we would like to warmly welcome you here."

I felt the sincerity in his voice, and when I remembered all the contempt and disdain that had been showered on me in the North, my throat went dry. I could not speak—I was so thankful that I was being treated truly like a human being.

When I finally gathered myself, I said, "Thank you so much for your kindness. I was up all night worrying about today because I was afraid that there might be a harsh interrogation. In the North, we were told terrible stories of people being interrogated and tortured in the South, but now I see how foolish I was in believing them."

Thus the interview began. The officials politely asked for an account of how I was captured, my life in the North, and how I had escaped. My story could not be told in just a few hours—I had so much to say. Instead, for the next few days, I recounted the past fifty years of my life to them.

When the debriefing was over, my interviewers took me out to a very nice restaurant, where they hosted a small party for me. There was so much delicious food! I had never seen or heard of many of the dishes that were served to us. I was moved by the dignified treatment I received from the interviewers. I had not made any major contribution to the country; I was just an old man. But they made me feel so welcome and appreciated here. I still feel nothing but gratitude toward them.

At the party, they told me, "Since you were officially listed as killed in action, there is a lot of paperwork to fill out in order to restore your identity.

Plus, we need to register you for a new identification card.[78] We suggest that you stay here with us, and in the meantime you can learn more about life in Korea."

The next day, a nice man named Mr. Chung came by and slowly began to teach me about Korean society. First, he took me to the veterans' hospital to get a general health checkup. Then, he took me on many tours of the city and taught me about how the world had changed since the Korean War. Every time we went out, I would be in a state of wonder at all the new and interesting things I saw. I had entered a whole new world.

When Mr. Chung took me to the War Memorial Museum, I was glad that he was able to verify my story. Back at the processing center, I had told my interviewers that I was captured in June of 1953 by the Chinese Army in the Gimhwa area of Gangwon Province, but they didn't really believe me. They thought that the Chinese didn't advance that far until July of that year, but Mr. Chung did some research, and found out that indeed the Chinese were there in June. My testimony was verified.

When I saw the grandeur of the city, it never ceased to amaze me that the South was extravagantly rich, while the North couldn't even keep its people from starving to death. It was clear to me now that the government in the North had purposefully neglected its people, so that Party members lived like kings, and everyone else was left to fend for themselves. Meanwhile, total control of the media ensured that many people in the North continued to believe that their society was better than the rest of the world, so, tragically, they worked hard and devoted their lives to a government that did not care about them.

First, I received my new ID card, and then on October 20, 2000, I was officially discharged from military duty. The day before the ceremony, on October 19, I had received my uniform from the ROK Army, 5th Division Headquarters. It was very moving to receive the uniform. I was so grateful that I would receive a full discharge ceremony from the Army that I could not sleep the night before.

At my discharge ceremony, my father, stepmother, stepbrothers, relatives, and friends were present. Wearing my new, neatly pressed uniform, I proudly entered the plaza. I felt honored to be wearing the uniform of the Republic of Korea Army. The staff officers and the division commander all came out and gave me a warm welcome.

---

[78] The South Korean Identification Number is similar to the Social Security number in the United States.

Soon more officers and servicemen poured into the plaza, and after the military anthem had been played, the discharge ceremony commenced. The division commander placed a wreath around my shoulders. I nervously reported to him, "Young-Bok Yoo, serial number 9395049, reporting for discharge." In that moment the faces of all my friends, colleagues, and fellow soldiers—the other POWs who had yet to return—flashed before my eyes.

I learned that even though I had not fought particularly well, I had been awarded the Hwarang Cordon[79] back in September, 1954. I had the pleasure of receiving that award at my discharge ceremony. I was a little embarrassed to receive such an award when, in my opinion, I had not done anything in particular to deserve such recognition.

I could not think of an instance when I had done something worthy of all this honor and praise; I was simply thankful to be alive and mindful of the sacrifice of innumerable, long-forgotten soldiers. They had bravely given their precious lives for their fatherland during the Korean War, fighting for scores of unnamed hills in Korea.

Now I was a true South Korean citizen. If I hadn't escaped, I would have remained just another casualty of the Korean War.

---

[79] The Order of Military Merit, 4th class, is awarded to soldiers who sacrificed their lives in combat.

34

Father

After the discharge ceremony, I went to live with my family. Now that I was a full-fledged Korean citizen, I could begin to lead a stable life. I spent a lot of time with my family and met many old friends. We had a lot of stories to share.

For a while, my father seemed to be in disbelief. He would often ask me, "Are you really Young-Bok—the one we thought was dead?" Then he would ask me about the times we had spent together. These questions helped me remember my own past. In particular, we remembered the day that he came to visit me at boot camp in Nonsan. It was the last time I had seen him in fifty years.

My father was so happy to chat with me, but some days, due to his dementia, he was not completely aware of himself. I wished that I had come earlier, but I was so thankful that he had endured this long so that I could see him.

I had my own room, but I shared it with my father because he wanted to sleep in the same room as me. We told a lot of stories. He wanted to hear about my mother and siblings in the North. It was especially difficult to tell him about the death of my mother, as well as my brother Young-Chul and my sister Myung-Sook. We cried a lot. He still felt guilty for sending my mother and siblings to Yeon-An. He blamed himself, and he prayed that war would never again come to the Korean Peninsula.

Though the stories I told him were sad, he said that he felt fortunate to hear at least some news about them.

My stepmother and my sister told me that my father never really accepted the loss of his family, and he had vowed to live long enough to be reunited with them one day. They said that this was why my father had lived for so long. It is certainly a blessing that we met. Had we not, he would have died never knowing what had become of his family.

Sadly, my father passed away six months after our reunion. He was ninety-four years old. It was as if he did not have to cling to life any longer now that I was back. I was in deep sorrow, but people at the funeral comforted me, saying that my father was surely resting in peace because his long lost son had returned.

35

On Repatriation

In the South, I finally learned what it is like to live in a truly free democracy, and I experienced free speech for the first time.[80] But of course it will be a long time before I am truly adjusted to the modern Korean lifestyle.

I lived most of my life in North Korea, but I think I learned more about the country while living in the South. In an isolated and authoritarian state, such as the North, all outside information is censored or cut off altogether, so I had no idea how backward and primitive North Korea was compared to its neighboring countries.

Here in the South, I have access to domestic as well as international news. It has been an awakening. I feel proud to be part of a strong and independent democratic nation, but there are some things that are very disappointing.

Ours is a free and dignified nation, and we must work to protect ourselves from the North and other outside threats, such as those that have troubled Korea in the past. The people must all fulfill their civic duties. Yet today there are many young men who try to dodge the draft and make up excuses so that they don't have to defend their country. Some even give

---

[80] During the author's childhood, from 1930-1945, Korea was under the harsh authoritarian rule of Imperial Japan, and from 1945 until 1948 South Korea was under US military rule. Although South Korean President Syngman Rhee was democratically elected in 1948 by popular vote, Rhee was also an authoritarian ruler. Rhee ruled South Korea until 1960. South Korea continued to be ruled by military dictators until 1987, when the people finally won free elections and free speech. When the author escaped to South Korea in 2000, it would have been his first experience living in a free society.

up citizenship and abandon their country, the same country where their ancestors are buried.

There are sad stories of greed. Legislators and other officials are reported to take bribes and fail their duty to lead the nation. Some siblings get in major fights and legal battles over their parents' estates. So much misery, disappointment, and trouble—just for money.

Many people hope for reunification. But before we focus on unifying Korea, we must first unify ourselves. How much longer will we argue and fight amongst ourselves over being liberal or conservative? I'm not saying we should stop debating and arguing completely. Debate and conflict is natural and essential in a democracy. But to me it seems so chaotic. The people must show more understanding and compassion toward one another.

It is unquestionable that South Koreans have achieved a great deal. Although some people worry that the gap between the rich and poor in South Korea is too great, anyone who is not disabled or too old can easily earn enough for a good living. Compared to North Korea, where it is impossible to advance if you are born to the "wrong" parents, such as a South Korean POW, South Korea is truly a land of opportunity. When I was hiding in China, I heard from many people who wanted to visit South Korea. This is probably the first time in history that people in Korea have enjoyed such prosperity. This is probably the first time in our history that Korea has become a place where even foreigners seek to come and build their dreams, rather than an impoverished country that people seek to leave.

However, it seems that people who lead comfortable lives, with no idea of the hardships endured by people in North Korea and other less fortunate countries, complain even more. I was surprised to learn how many people in South Korea are unhappy and even commit suicide. As a survivor of famine and oppression in North Korea, I want to tell them to just keep on trying. I hope they persevere in their efforts to overcome their individual ordeals, no matter how difficult the struggle may seem. I also hope they overcome their despair, and that my own survival may help such people see that life is worth living, no matter how bleak things may appear at the moment.

There are countless South Korean POWs who have been oppressed, exploited, and enslaved. But they always believed that one day, before they died, they would return to their home. They have waited for this day, enduring hardship after hardship, in hopes that one day they would be free. The majority died without ever seeing that day. But their desire to return home is still present. It was the last wish of many prisoners to be buried in the fatherland one day.

Even if we cannot reunify the country, our government must do everything in its power to bring home the remains of our POWs. Also, we must rescue the children of these POWs who live in oppression in the North. That is the only way that the country can take full responsibility for its soldiers, who laid down their lives for the good of the nation.

36

They Lived in Hell

Most POWs experienced unending troubles in North Korea. Many passed away in poverty, misery, and neglect after years of unrewarded toil. POWs were considered slaves. Countless numbers of them died in needless accidents, and countless more died of disease. The fortunate ones who survived these trials faced further discrimination. People who resisted or even complained about the inequality were taken away to camps for political prisoners or beaten nearly to death, only to die slowly from their wounds. Thus many years passed and many prisoners of war passed away.

When my POW construction brigade was disbanded in 1956, most POWs were sent to work at the Kumduck or Ryong-Yang Mines, but a few were also sent to work in other industrial sectors. For example, Ho-Kun Jang and Ho-Gwon Kim were sent to work on farms. Sang-Ho Byun was sent to work at an opium farm,[81] the largest one in North Korea. Others, such as Ho-Kun Jang and Ho-Gwon Kim, were sent to work on regular farms.

In spite of all the struggles and discrimination the POWs faced, many studied hard in hopes of gaining recognition and eventual Party membership by becoming skilled laborers. They included Jae-Sool Park, Dae-Sung Kang, Jong-Hwan Gu, Yong-Bong Kim, Sung-Gyu Choi, Bong-Do Lee, and Tae-Hyung Chun. They studied with me at the Kumduck technical

---

[81] Desperate to acquire foreign currency, the North Korean government has resorted to exporting narcotics, such as opium, to China.

school in various trades. Some of us actually succeeded in making it into the Party, including Hyuk-Gun Yang, Jae-Sool Park, Tae-Hyun Chun, Hyung-Shik Kang, and Bok-Am Choi.

One case stands out as unique. Joo-Suk Yang got married to a respectable woman surveyor named Oak-Hi Li. Mr. Yang was a very talented surveyor himself and was honored as a "workers' committee productivity leader." His skills got him admitted to the Party. Li, herself a Party member, had graduated from a prestigious surveying technical school. The two made a model couple. They were happily married and had two children.

Yang had a lot of potential, so the Workers' Committee sent him up to the Pyongyang offices for further training. Oak-Hi stayed behind and lived comfortably off the money Yang sent her from Pyongyang. But even the luckiest did not make it. One day, without warning, Oak-Hi lost all contact with her husband. She stopped receiving money and letters from him. The Party Committee at the mine could not explain what had happened to him. With no support, she had to go back to her sister's place. We later heard a rumor that Yang had been sent to the South as a spy but did not return.[82]

On the other hand, there were many student enlistees who, like me, had been conscripted into the North Korean Army. I had deserted the North before joining the South Korean Army, but there were many conscripts who remained with the North Korean forces. These soldiers were treated well.

The Party took a great interest in these young veterans, telling them that when the communist reunification of the Korean peninsula was complete, they would be appointed administrators and governors in the South. This was not entirely an empty promise. Plans were drawn up in preparation for the communist reunification, and according to these plans, some trusted veterans were in line to manage specific towns, villages, and cities. Many were sent to the People's Economics University at Song-Do and were paid to research and prepare for reunification, but it remains unclear whether these plans would ultimately have been followed.

---

[82] This rumor is questionable. The North Korean government uses the family of a spy to tether him to the North. When a spy is actively working in the South, his or her family is treated well. Should he be killed or captured, his family will be treated like heroes, but if he defects, his family will be severely punished. This makes it highly unlikely that Yang became a spy, since if he had become a spy, his wife and children would either be pampered or punished, but not neglected, like Oak-Hi.

There are also many South Korean soldiers who had defected to the North Korean Army. These "old veterans" were taken care of by the state. Many were inducted into the Party and afforded as much respect as regular soldiers.

Ironically, student enlistees of the North Korean Army who had been captured and interned by UN forces, and then chosen to be repatriated to the North, were treated poorly. One of my neighbors, Gu-Chan Chung, was one of these returning veterans. He was born in Choong-Chung Province, sixty miles south of Seoul. When the war broke out, he was conscripted into the North Korean Army. Then, like me, he was captured and held at the Koje-Do POW Camp. While I asked to be returned to the South, he chose to be repatriated to the North, but in the North he was treated like a traitor because he had surrendered rather than fight to the death. The government seemed to be very suspicious of these repatriated soldiers. They could not tell if the soldier had returned of his own volition, or on the instructions of a South Korean spy agency. Chung, who had chosen to be repatriated to the North of his own free will, tragically spent the remainder of his life as a laborer at the Dong-Am Mine.

On the opposite end of the spectrum were the regular soldiers of the North Korean Army. These were praised and celebrated by the government. In the 1990 War Veteran Commemoration ceremonies, all living North Korean war veterans were given "Veteran's Medals" and a war bonus. Also, on July 27 of every year, the day of the ceasefire, North Korea holds a victory ceremony,[83] and many veterans are given an extra bag of rice on that day.

Officially, the POWs were called "war veterans," too, and back when we were first released from the construction brigades, we were also promised that we would be treated just like any other North Korean citizen. Unfortunately the reality could not have been further from the truth. We were constantly kept under surveillance, restricted, and discriminated against. The POW label followed us like a shadow until we died. But this label was not public. Often, a younger worker who was unaware that I was a prisoner of war would ask me why I did not receive any medals or participate in any of the veterans' ceremonies even though I was a "war veteran." Whenever this question arose, I would be at a loss for words.

---

[83] The North proclaims the ceasefire as a "victory."

37

Stories

From time to time I meet with other POWs who have escaped the North. I've learned that others overcame far greater hardships than me. Here are their stories:

Jin-Hwan Jang was captured in December, 1951, in Gangwon Province, near the present-day DMZ. He spent a few months doing odd tasks at a North Korean People's Army (KPA) base. When the North Korean Army was running low on troops, he and other POWs were sent to the front to fight the South Korean soldiers. The POWs didn't want to betray the South, even at gunpoint. A captured South Korean officer secretly organized a small group of sixty POWs and North Korean defectors who wanted to escape. The sixty soldiers tried to fight their way to the South Korean lines, but they ran into an entire battalion of troops just 150 meters from freedom. They were all captured and sentenced to death by firing squad. Jin-Hwan Jang and one other POW were spared execution because of their youth. Instead, they were sentenced to twenty years in prison. The remaining fifty-eight escapees were executed.

Jang was sent to Shinuiju Prison. After serving seventeen years, his sentence was commuted, and he was "released" to work in the mines. Years later, he attempted to escape again, but was captured once again and sentenced to six more years in prison. After being released, he continued to work in the mines until he retired. In retirement, he constantly searched for a way to escape from the North, and in early 2000, he finally got away.

I have a great deal of respect for him. Every time he was knocked down, he got back up and tried again.

Pil-Suk Kim was captured by the North and assigned to a North Korean Army unit. He tried to escape in 1953, but was caught and sentenced to thirteen years in prison. After his release, he was sent to work at the Juwon coalmine, in North Hamgyong Province. He escaped the country successfully in 2001.

Chul-Shik Kim has also led a sad and difficult life. He worked at the Onsong Mine in North Hamgyong Province. His wife died when he was very young, so eventually he had to live with his son. But his son died as well, so he had to live with his daughter-in-law. Luckily, his daughter-in-law treated him well, and thanks to her efforts he was able to cross the Tumen River to freedom around the same time as I. We met at the POW processing center in South Korea, where we were both staying. Perhaps because of the hard mine labor, he shakes when he tries to pick up anything, even something as light as a spoon. He has trouble eating on his own, and often needs to be fed.

Sang-Doo Oh, now eighty-two, enlisted in the ROK Army in August of 1951, leaving behind his wife and three children in the South. He also has a moving story. After his capture, he was ordered to work at the Hakpo coalmine, where he met a North Korean woman, married her, and remained with her for fifty years. However, they were unable to have children. When they got old, Sang-Doo felt depressed. He began to miss his family in the South greatly, and often spoke of this to his wife. His wife was very understanding. She told him that she had lived with him happily for fifty years and wanted him to be happy. She helped him escape, and in 2004 he made it to the South. Oh was joyfully reunited with his first wife and his now grown-up children.

Chul-Soo Kim was serving with the ROK Army Capital Division,[84] when he was captured and sent to the Hoeryeong prison camp. He got sick and could not open his eyes or move. The other prisoners thought he had died, so they prepared to bury him. But just before they covered him up, he awakened, and they discovered he was still barely alive. He slowly recovered and worked in the mines until he escaped. He later got his wife out of North Korea, and the two are living happily now in the South.

---

[84] The Capital Division of the ROK Army is in charge of protecting Seoul, the capital of South Korea.

It's nearly impossible to escape the North on your own. Everyone who escapes has a broker or guide who helps them. I wanted to help my friend **Sung-Tek Cheon**, who lived with me at Kumduck Mine, to escape, so I contacted the brokers who had brought me to the South, and they managed to liberate him successfully. When he arrived in Korea we had a very emotional reunion, and his brothers in the South personally thanked me for my help.

We also tried to get another one of my friends from Kumduck out of North Korea: **Sung-chae Jung**, who had a wife and a son in the South. Unfortunately we failed to get him out. But we were able to get news about Sung-Chae to his son, Kyoung-Ju, and his wife, who had not seen him in decades.

Many of the POWs who make it home still suffer from depression. They feel guilty for leaving their wives and children in North Korea and have difficulty getting along with people in the South because of such pain. However, we are all grateful to have been able to escape from the hell of North Korea, even in our old age. We consider ourselves lucky compared to the countless POWs who were senselessly killed in North Korea. Too many of us were executed unjustly.

Several POWs were executed when they resisted the North Korean government and sought repatriation. **Young-Sang Choi** openly protested and demonstrated his desire for repatriation, so he was publicly executed as an example to the other POWs. This did not deter **Myung-Dal Bek**. He and five other prisoners organized a bomb plot, using mining explosives. Their plan to blow up a mineshaft was discovered, and they, too, were publically executed.

The North Korean government was ruthless. They executed any protester or dissenter publicly, so they would be an example to the other POWs. However, many prisoners would become so frustrated that they would protest anyway, and they were executed as a result.

Many of the POWs were sent to the infamous penal labor camps. **Soo-Young Hong**, who had been a ROK Army Sergeant, died in the Yoduk Penal Labor Camp in 2006. His son, **Yon-Joong**, who escaped from North Korea, revealed there were many ROK Army officers in Yoduk. One of the officers was **Bong-Cheol Park**. Park told Yon-Joong that one day the North Koreans executed many of the officers. He told Yon-Joong that he thought the Yoduk authorities were going to kill him and the few other South Korean officers who had not been executed as well. I thought it must have been terribly painful for Park to tell that story and also painful for Yon-Joong to hear it.

Sergeant **Kum-Yong Sohn** was another POW who protested against his treatment. The State Security agents took Sohn away and tortured him. Sohn died in prison. There was **Sergeant Seok-Yong Kim** and **First Lieutenant Jong-Hoon Lee**, both of whom died in a penal labor camp.

There was also a village near Ryong-Moon coalmine in North Hamgyong Province where several dozen former officer POWs lived. There was a rumor that the officer POWs were all taken away one night and were never heard from again. This kind of disappearance was said to happen if the authorities made you work on a secret military construction project. The workers would be killed after the work was finished.

These sad stories are only revealed to us through the testimonies of escaped POWs. There are undoubtedly countless POWs who were killed and buried without leaving a trace behind. Countless more committed suicide.

But the government in the North is cruel even to people who take their own lives. When someone commits suicide, the government opens a big investigation, and even interrogates family members. It is considered an act of betrayal if you commit suicide in the "paradise" created with such care by Kim Il-Sung and Kim Jong-Il. People who kill themselves in the political prison camps still have to serve their prison sentences: their bodies are buried within the grounds of the prison. Even in death they cannot rest in peace.

Many prisoners so desire to return to their homeland in the South that their last request is to be buried in the South. I hope that one day their children will be able to return the remains of their parents to the South, so that these prisoners may finally rest in peace.

Some prisoners escaped, thanks to the fierce devotion of their relatives in South Korea.

The **Lee brothers** (they declined to give their real names), who lived in South Korea, had believed that their father was killed in the Korean War. One day they received a letter supposedly written by him.

At first they doubted the authenticity of the letter and asked South Korea's Ministry of Unification to help confirm whether or not their father was alive in the North. They discovered that their father was indeed living in North Korea.

They applied for one of the Red Cross-sponsored North-South family reunions, in which family members that have been separated by the war have an opportunity to see each other. Two years later a reunion was granted, and so the brothers were finally able to meet their father at the Mount Kumkang "Separated Family Meeting Center" in September of 2003. After a very moving reunion, the three brothers quietly persuaded their father to escape the North. The next year, he successfully escaped and now lives with his sons.

Sung-Min Shin, another South Korean, found out that his brother, who was thought to have perished in the Korean War, was alive in the North. He spent a lot of his own money in an effort to rescue him. The brokers managed to get him to China, where the brothers met for the first time in decades. However, the Chinese police found them, revoked their passports, and threw them in jail for twenty days. When Shin was released, he found out that his brother had been pressured by the Chinese police into telling reporters that he would return to North Korea. Luckily, Shin managed to convince his brother that going back would be suicidal, and contacted the South Korean consulate. The consulate helped the two safely reach South Korea.

Other prisoners make it all the way to China, but they do not get any help from their relatives in the South, so they never make it home.

A 76-year-old prisoner in the North Hamgyong Province wanted to return home so dearly that he escaped to China on his own. In China he contacted a broker and asked him to find his nephew on Jeju Island, in South Korea. The broker found the nephew, but the nephew did not have the money required to get his uncle from China to Korea, so the prisoner had no choice but to return to the North.

Another prisoner managed to escape to China with his wife, but the brokers could not get in contact with his family in the South. He waited for six months with no word until North Korean agents in China discovered and captured him. They were about to take him back when he killed himself. He knew that he was doomed either way.

Prisoners risk their lives to make it to the South, but too many of them die attempting to escape.

On January 27, 2005, the Korean news reported that a POW named **Man-Tek Han** had made it to China, but before he could meet with his relatives he was captured by Chinese police and sent back to the North. What was worse, the South Korean government did not find out about this until a month after Han was sent back. His family was so angry that they returned all of his medals to the government. They were disgusted that the South Korean government could not even rescue Han when he had made it all the way to China on his own.

Some prisoners make it all the way to the South and yet still cannot find peace because they are worried for their families in the North.

Many prisoners feel extremely guilty about leaving family members in the North. We are always burdened by the guilt that we caused our children to suffer and thus failed to do our duty as parents. Even before we escape, our children suffer from discrimination and mistreatment because of their father's POW status. Once we escape, the North Korean authorities sometimes interrogate and punish family members. Life becomes worse for the children of escaped POWs. Even though we are free in South Korea, we are heartbroken that we have failed our children again.

Some of the prisoners have managed to retrieve their families as well, but the majority have traveled alone like me or brought only a few family members with them. Upon arrival in the South, prisoners try to rescue the family members that they left behind, but it is usually much harder since the North Korean authorities increase surveillance.

I knew when I left that retrieving my whole family would be impossible. I try not to give myself false hope because it would be pointless and probably just make things worse. But I still try to save as much money as I can in case I ever get a chance to help them. They are always on my mind, but as of now there is nothing I can do for them.

In the year 2000, my friend **Young-Jun Park**, who worked with me at the Kumduck and Dong-Am mines, spent a lot of money trying to rescue his wife and children, but the attempt failed. Later, his youngest son, **Jung-Gi Park**, escaped to China with Young-Jun's granddaughter. In China they were in the midst of boarding a ship headed for Korea when they were caught by the Chinese police and turned over to the North. Young-Jun was crushed.

A while later, he learned that his family had been exiled to a remote labor camp where they were struggling to survive. Since hearing of the state of his family, he has been in constant misery. He can do nothing but anxiously hope for reunification of North and South, so that he can rescue them.

Moon-Ja Lee, who escaped in 2004, made a great effort to bring his family to the South. Out of his twelve children and grandchildren, his brokers planned to retrieve his daughter, his youngest son, and his youngest son's family—a group of eight. Recently, he went to China to meet them as soon as they crossed the Tumen River. Everything was set and Moon-Ja even got a call saying that his family was leaving. Tragically, they were caught just before they entered the broker's van. All eight of them were arrested and punished. And it got worse: the authorities also arrested Moon-Ja's elder son, even though he had not participated because he did not report his brother to the police. He, too, was punished.

When Moon-Ja found out, he was distraught with grief. He wrote letters of complaint to the Korean government and to the Ministry of Unification. He came over to my place one day and showed me the replies he had received. He also plans to write to the American government. He is angry that after the Korean War, the UN Army made sure that all of the foreign troops were repatriated, but the South Korean soldiers, who were also fighting under the UN banner, were simply abandoned. How could they ignore the South Korean POWs and allow so many of them to be oppressed and enslaved?

Yong-Woo Kim, who escaped in 2004, asked brokers to bring his wife and youngest son out of North Korea. The brokers agreed, and in February of 2005, he gave them a large sum of money. The brokers succeeded bring Yong-Woo's family to China. Unfortunately the brokers betrayed Yong-Woo and the family. Yong-Woo learned that the Chinese Police were offering a reward of 10,000 Yuan (US $1,500) for any information on escapees from North Korea. The shameless brokers only cared about money and turned over the family to the Chinese police.

The Chinese police turned Yong-Woo's wife and son over to the North Koreans. Yong-Woo's son was taken to the Musan State Security Headquarters where he was tortured and killed. Yong-Woo has not heard from his wife and has nowhere to turn for help. Due to the tragic loss of his son and wife, Yong-Woo Kim suffers unbearable pain and agony. Unless the POW issue is resolved soon, he will never be able to come out of his misery.

A leading figure in the fight to repatriate the POWs is **Thomas Yong-Bong Chung**. During the Korean War, Chung was a company commander in the 8th division of the ROK Army, assigned to the Yangku region in Gangwon Province. Many of his soldiers were taken prisoner during fierce combat in that region. After the war, he went to the United States, where he became a successful businessman. Today he still works tirelessly to free his men as the leader of the Korean War POW Affairs – USA in Los Angeles, a nongovernmental organization that advocates for South Korean POWs.

There were many prisoners of war as a result of the Korean War. After the ceasefire and the armistice agreement, international law states that all POWs should be repatriated. That never happened, and though nobody is sure exactly how many POWs there are, it is clear that there are far too many. The Communists captured 10,000 UN soldiers and 70,000 ROK soldiers during the war. Almost all of the UN soldiers who survived captivity were returned, but only 8,000 South Korean soldiers were repatriated, leaving 62,000 prisoners behind. Other estimates say that "only" 19,000 were never returned. Either way, the exact numbers are irrelevant. It is clear that there was a large number of South Korean POWs who were oppressed and enslaved in the North. There are at least eighty live witnesses, POWs like myself who have escaped from North Korea.

All the prisoners were forced to work as slaves in the mines until they got old or died. Now many are so old that they cannot support themselves. They live not knowing whether the next day is the day they will die.

Still, the North claims that they have no POWs. How can we just let the issue slide so easily? Why are there so few people in South Korea who sincerely care about the plight of the POWs? And when will the Korean government finally take responsibility for its soldiers and bring home its POWs? The Republic of Korea cannot consider itself a proud and sovereign nation until it can bring its soldiers home.

A nation's strength is not simply determined by its economy or by its military. It is not determined by the way it treats its citizens during prosperous times. No, a nation's strength is determined by the way it treats the young men it sends to the front lines during a time of crisis. Those men made sacrifices for their country's survival. Now the country must return the favor.

The United States, to this day, continues working to recover the remains of its soldiers who died in the North. They are still looking for their fallen and will not stop until all of their missing soldiers are accounted for. The United States will go to the ends of the earth to bring home the remains of troops who laid down their lives in her defense. Yet Korea cannot even retrieve her living soldiers, whose sacrifices have certainly been as great as the Americans.

The Japanese prime minister personally made two trips to the North to guarantee the return of a few Japanese civilians kidnapped by the North. He showed that the nation was ready to go to any lengths for the safety of its people. The whole country was interested and devoted to the cause. When I see such dedication, I am disheartened by the callousness shown by the Korean public and the government.

In October of 2000, the South Korean government freed and repatriated to North Korea sixty-three agents and pro-North Korean activists. These old men had been serving sentences in South Korean prisons for decades. The North proclaimed these returning prisoners as heroic patriots. I do not question the humanitarian gesture by the South Korean government, but why did the government not demand the return of our own POWs?

It is correct for the South Korean government to welcome and hold ceremonies for POWs who escape on their own. But this is the bare minimum of what the government can do to support the POWs. They should be proactive in pressing for the repatriation of the prisoners. Even North Korea takes responsibility for its men. Why can't we do the same?

No matter how much the North denies holding any prisoners of war, we have real evidence. Over eighty prisoners have made it to back to the South to bear witness. If the government made a strong effort, I am sure we could find a solution to the prisoner of war issue.

The North held on to the South Korean POWs primarily to use as labor for postwar reconstruction. The North also hoped enough of the POWs would join their cause and use their knowledge of the South to assist the Northern dream of communist reunification. But now, after the POWs have been thoroughly exploited, they are all old and no longer valuable to the government. The North has no reason to hold onto these prisoners. Of course, it may be embarrassing for North Korean leaders to admit that they lied. But if we work hard enough, we should be able to find a way for both sides to save face. Both sides claim to want peace and reconciliation. We must find a way not to blame and shame each other for resolving the POW issue is a necessary step for true peace.

Granted, the government does have a lot of work to do and a lot of pressing issues to resolve. But the POW problem is also a very urgent matter. We have to rescue them while they are still alive, if we want to shed more light on the fate of all prisoners and bring joy to the families.

Soldiers will also feel more confident knowing that their government will be responsible and bring them home. So, we cannot afford to delay in confronting this issue any longer, lest it become an issue of the past.

This is what I would like the Korean government to do about the POW issue:

First, I would like the government to try to bring back all of the POWs who wish to return as soon as possible. I am sure that the majority of POWs have a deep and strong desire to return to their homeland. However, most of them now have families and even grandchildren in the North. There may be many who decide to spend their last years with their families and friends in the North. A few POWs may have become Party members and may consider the North to be their home. Therefore, I hope the South Korean government can deal with the issue of repatriation based upon the individual choice of the POWs.

Second, and perhaps more urgently, I would like the government to focus upon improving the quality of life for POWs in the North, whether or not we can bring them home. Many are old and weak, and their bodies are beginning to fail. Their children do not have the resources to support them because their children also suffer persecution. They and their families are treated as the lowest caste in North Korean society. We must find a way to relieve their immediate suffering.

Whether we fully repatriate them or support them in the North, this will be a daunting task. The North may not be receptive to these ideas. However, the South has made a humanitarian gesture by returning the long-term communist prisoners. I am sure that the North-South relationship is improving. With a little more determination and sincerity by both governments, these goals are achievable.

It has been nearly ten years since I returned to the South. I've done the best I can to remember the names and the lives of the sixty or so POWs that I have mentioned in the book. I want to try to find their relatives in the South, but so far I have only managed to meet with three families. To this day, many POWs risk their lives trying to escape, and not all of them make it. Why do they take such huge risks in order to escape? It isn't simply because life in North Korea is so difficult. It isn't simply because they want to live out the rest of their lives in a nicer world with their families. No, they are risking their lives to escape the North because they are afraid of being *forgotten*. Being ignored and forgotten by the North is not nearly as terrifying as being ignored and forgotten by the South, our home. We can endure any struggle, overcome any hardship, and bear any burden, as long as our tragic story is remembered.

To be forgotten is worse than dying. There is truly nothing worse than not being remembered by *anyone*. It is as if you never existed. The South Korean POWs struggle to escape because they are afraid that the memories of them will turn to dust. We escape to remind the world, "We are still here! Please don't forget about us!"

I hear such voices every day. I hear the voices from my fellow POWs who died toiling in North Korean mines and from those who died trying to escape.

North and South Korea have slowly been improving relations. The separated family reunions have continued. But we do not hear one word about helping the POWs or their families. I have made it my mission to tell the stories of the POWs and make sure that we are not forgotten.

My generation, the generation that fought in the Korean War, is growing old. We are now in our seventies and eighties. Future generations will probably learn about the Korean War in history class. They will see photos of the separated families and the South Korean POWs, but it will feel as remote as wars that were fought centuries ago. But while the POWs are still alive, while I am still alive, the POW issue lives on in the present. It is not yet history; it is part of the now. These are my memories, which I want to reveal to the world, and make sure the memory of the South Korean POWs lives on.

Independent Evidence for the Existence of South Korean POWs

Aside from the testimony of eighty escaped POWs, the existence of South Korean POWs is further confirmed by new evidence from declassified Soviet Foreign Ministry Archives. In a paper titled *Armistice Talks in Korea (1951-1953) Based on Documents from the Russian Foreign Policy Archives*, historian Alena Volokhova says Soviet Ambassador to North Korea S.P. Suzdalev reported in a May 1953 memo that the North Koreans were holding "thousands" of South Koreans soldiers and forcing them to do hard labor for the government.

In a separate memo, Soviet diplomat Nikolai Fedorenko (who would later become the USSR representative to the UN Security Council) reported on a December 3, 1953 meeting between Kim Il-Sung and Mao Zedong. Kim and Mao talked about the POW issue. Mao was worried that the large number of South Korean POWs who were not returned would be revealed. Kim reassured them that the prisoners would be sent to remote northern mining regions of the country, where they would not be discovered and could not escape. As a result of this decision, the POWs were sent to the locations outlined in Appendix B.

The POW Construction Brigades

From 1953 until 1956, South Korean POWs were assigned to Interior Ministry Construction Brigades and put to work in various mines. In 1956, the Construction Brigades were disbanded, and the POWs were forcefully co-opted into the general population of the mines.

The chart below summarizes the specific mines and locations where the POW Construction Brigades were assigned to work.

Brigade	Sent to
1701	North Hamgyong Province: Ah Oh Ji Coalmine, Eunduk Coalmine, Oh-Bong Coalmine
1702	North Hamgyong Province: Hakpo Coalmine
1703	North Hamgyong Province: Hakpo Coalmine
1704	North Hamgyong Province: Hamyun Coalmine
1705	North Hamgyong Province: Hamyun Coalmine
1706	South Pyongan Province: Sung-Chun Mine
1707	South Hamgyong Province: Ryong-Yang Mine, Kumduck Mine
1708	South Hamgyong Province: Ryong-Yang Mine, Kumduck Mine
1709	North Hamgyong Province: Kokonwon Coalmine, Onsung Coalmine

Made in the USA
Lexington, KY
01 November 2012